EX AUDITU

An International Journal of Theological Interpretation of Scripture

Volume 7 1991

Ex Auditu is published annually by Pickwick Publications, 4137 Timberlane Drive, Allison Park, Pennsylvania 15101-2932, U.S.A.

Subscriptions
- Individuals:
  - U.S.A. - $15.00
  - Canada - $12.00 (in U.S. Funds)
  - All other countries - $15.00 (in U.S. Funds)
  - Students - $10.00
- Institutions:
  - U.S.A. - $25.00
  - Canada - $20.00 (in U.S. Funds)
  - All other countries - $25.00 (in U.S. Funds)

Indexed in *Religion Index One: Periodicals*, published by the American Theological Library Association, Chicago, Illinois, available online in the ATLA Religion Database through BRS Information Technologies (Latham, New York); DIALOGUE Information Services (Palo Alto, California); *Internationale Zeitschriftenshau für Bibelwissenschaft und Grenzgebeite; Religious and Theological Abstracts*; and *Old Testament Abstracts.*

Please address all subscription correspondence and change of address information to Pickwick Publications.

ISSN 08883-0053

EX AUDITU

An international journal of theological interpretation of scripture

THE EDITORIAL BOARD MEMBERS AND CONSULTANTS represent various disciplines and denominations. Theological Interpretation of Scripture is a task to be taken seriously by scholars who are committed to the Christian faith and tradition. However, as one editorial consultant stated: "let people gradually get used to the idea that a sane hermeneutics is both oriented in advance toward agreement/consent and is simultaneously exigent, discriminating, critical."

SPECIAL NOTICE

Pickwick Publications express their gratitude to Dr. Donald G. Miller for assuming the responsibility for editing this issue. We are also pleased to announce that Dr. Klyne Snodgrass has accepted the editorship of EX AUDITU as of Volume 8, 1992.

In Memoriam

ROBERT A. GUELICH

June 20, 1939 - July 3, 1991

The death of Robert A. Guelich on July 3, 1991 took away from the Church and the world of scholarship a genuine person gifted with a deep concern for the Scriptures and a relevant theology. He was deeply committed to the laity of the Church and to the students preparing for the ministry. At the time of his death he was Professor of New Testament at Fuller Theological Seminary where he joined the Faculty in the Fall of 1988. This was also the period when he assumed the position of Editor of EX AUDITU.

The annual Symposium on Theological Interpretation of Scripture was established on the campus of North Park Theological Seminary primarily due to the mutual respect and friendship between Bob and the administrative members of North Park College and Seminary.

As one reads the materials from the Fuller Seminary community that were written expressing their great sense of loss in the death of a great teacher who served not even four years, one is not surprised at all for we as members of the Editorial Board and as Editorial Consultants, share that sense of loss but remain ever grateful for the few years he served as Editor.

We convey our deep sympathies to Joyce, his wife and to their children in the loss of a husband and father and to Fuller Theological Seminary in their loss of a member of their faculty. In their invitation to join the Fuller community at their service of remembrance we find a statement which speaks also to our own situation."Dr. Guelich's untimely death is an incalculable loss to the Fuller community and to the Christian world. The fruits of his many years of research in the fields of Gospel Studies and Christology reflected not only in his teaching and scholarly writing, but in a profound way, in his personal life and his pastoral concern for all with whom he came in contact."

It is proper that we share a brief paragraph from Bob Guelich's Commentary on the Sermon on the Mount. "Blessed are those who mourn. There is little in our experience today that reveals more our ultimate lack of control, our insufficiency, our ultimate dependency on Someone greater than ourselves, than the experience of mourning. Regardless of whether our mourning takes the shape of anger, grief, or remorse, it betrays our vulnerability and sense of helplessness. Our only hope lies beyond our own capacities. The restoration that brings true comfort must come from the Comforter himself."

EX AUDITU

Volume 7 1991

In Memoriam

Robert A. Guelich

CONTENTS

INTRODUCTION

The task of theology is increasingly difficult. The multitude of publications and issues forces theologians to overspecialization. The academic context of much theological work tends to cloud the nature and purpose of the enterprise. Too frequently theological work becomes the history of theology, a chronicling of academic work on the subject, or continual effort to protect one's academic reputation. As a result, theology and its significance for life do not find the light of day. Concern for the life of the Church is forgotten. North Park's Symposium on the Theological Interpretation of Scripture and EX AUDITU seek to provide a context whereby scholars are encouraged to do theology *for the Church.* Even in such a context, scholars find it difficult to abandon their usual practice or to focus broadly enough for their contributions to be of assistance to the Church.

Current Christological discussions are a primary example of the diversion of theology from its task. As Leander Keck pointed out, New Testament Christology often is really the history of Christological materials and motifs. In particular, the focus on Christological titles has tended to distort and hamper Christological reflection. What is needed is an explicitly theological approach to New Testament Christology which will show the identity and significance of Jesus.[1]

Although it may be a truism, Christology is the focus and basis of Christianity. That is not to suggest some type of "christomonism," for other theological topics, especially theology proper, are Important as well. All other theological topics. however, are understood in light of the significance of Jesus and his work. Christianity affirms that in Jesus of Nazareth God and his purposes are most clearly perceived. No simple Christology will do, for the New Testament gives evidence of a variety of Christologies. The various christologies are like facets of a diamond: each may be analyzed individually, but all must be taken together for a full appreciation.

Christological treatises usually find their climax in consideration of the Incarnation. Recent discussions about the origin of the idea of Incarnation have only intensified the debate.[2] The early church, however, either did not see or did not value the difficulties that moderns have with the subject. Early Christians were convinced that in encountering Jesus they had encountered God working out his purposes for humanity. We ought not forget that christology has its foundation in the *experience of Jesus*, rather than in thoughts about Jesus.[3]

The breadth of the issues involved in a discussion of Christology and Incarnation precludes a comprehensive treatment in this journal. Instead, each of the participants in the symposium treats Incarnation from the perspective of a specific subject in his or her discipline. James Luther Mays and Ralph Klein both deal with the contribution of the Hebrew scriptures to the discussion of Christology. In addition, Balmer Kelly's article "Word of Promise: The Incarnation in the Old Testament," originally published in *Interpretation,*

X (1956), 3-15, is reprinted here. Howard Marshall and Tom Wright both discuss aspects of New Testament Christology, the former focusing on "Son of Man" and the latter showing how Paul applied Christology to the problem of living in a pagan world. Fred Norris shows how Athanasius and Gregory of Nazianzus functioned with Scripture when discussing the Incarnation. Larry Murphy shows how African Americans have formed a Christology for living. Colin Brown tackles issues of how Incarnation and trinity are to be understood. The article by Molly Marshall was originally a sermon delivered at the worship service of the symposium. As expected. the participants at times disagreed, but the articles betray a general consensus that, while classical formulations are valuable, something more needs to be said. These articles are steps on the way to that "something more," a theology of the Incarnation which, as Tom Wright points out, show us how to live in a pagan world. To each of the authors we express our gratitude.

The schedule for future symposia is as follows:

October 9-11, 1992	Worship
October 8-10, 1993	Resurrection
October 7-9, 1994	The Church

For information about attending, please write Ms. Nancy Fisher, North Park Theological Seminary, 3225 W. Foster, Chicago, IL 60625.

Klyne Snodgrass
Editor

NOTES

1. Leander E. Keck, "Toward the Renewal of New Testament Christology." *New Testament Studies*. XXXII (1986), 362 and 368-370.

2. Note James D. G. Dunn, *Christology in the Making: A New Testament Inquiry into the Origins of the Doctrine of the Incarnation* (Philadelphia: Westminster Press, 1980), who argues that no antecedents exist that explain the origin of the doctrine of the Incarnation. His book is at least partially a response to the British discussions of Incarnation and myth. Dunn added fuel to the debate by denying any concept of preexistence to New Testament writers other than the evangelist of the fourth gospel and, to some extent, the writer of Hebrews. However, his treatments of the relevant Pauline texts are deficient.

3. See the similar argument in Larry Murphy's reflections on "African American Perspectives on Christology and Incarnation," pp. 73-82 below.

"In A Vision"[1]
The Portrayal of the Messiah in the Psalms

JAMES LUTHER MAYS

> "No Christ could validate himself as the disclosure of a hidden divine sovereignty over history or as a vindication of the meaningfulness of history, if a Christ were not expected" (Reinhold Niebuhr).[2]

> "Jesus is what he is only in the context of Israel's expectation. Without the background of this tradition, Jesus would never have become the object of a Christology" (Wolfhart Pannenberg).[3]

I. INTRODUCTION

The above observations from theologians of the past and present generations affirm the importance of the Old Testament for the career of Jesus and the project of Christology. Both speak of the Old Testament and the traditions of Israel which it transmits in terms of "expectation." The Old Testament texts do not speak about Jesus of Nazareth, at least in readings that will pass muster in our modern intellectual climate. The Jesus of history was not there as reference for these texts. But some of these texts do speak about YHWH, God of Israel and the world, and of YHWH's way with Israel and the world, through and in the Messiah of God. In that sense, there is a knowledge of the Messiah-Christ in the Old Testament. The claims of these theologians reflect the confession implied by the biblical canon of the Old Testament and the New Testament that Jesus is not known as Christ apart from the knowledge of the Christ/Messiah of the Old Testament. What the Old Testament says about the Messiah is prolegomena; only from the New Testament do we hear the legomena. The Old Testament provides a description of the person and role of the Christ that is personified by Jesus in an enactment that revises and transcends the description. But it is from the Old Testament that we know the description that is revised and transcended.

When the particular topic of Christology is Incarnation as a specific mode of relation between God and Jesus, the movement between the Old Testament and the New Testament witness is narrowed and focused. The Old Testament speaks of the Christ; it does not speak directly of incarnation. The possible connections between such texts as John 1:14 and Proverbs 8 and Philippians 2:5-11 and Isaiah 53 have been explored and discussed thoroughly. What the Psalms say, however, about YHWH's relation to the

Messiah of God does have implications for the particular topic, as well as for Christology in general.

II. THE APPROACH

What is proposed here is to follow the direction given in the accounts of Jesus' inaugural baptism. Christology as theological work begins with Jesus and the question of the relation between Jesus and God. The baptismal accounts testify that at the beginning of his ministry, a divine word quoted from Psalm 2 was spoken to and about Jesus: "You are my son" (Mark 1:11 and parallels). The second psalm is the first of a group of psalms in the Psalter that contains the most substantive and coherent testimony to the relation between God and the Messiah of God in the Old Testament, though of course not the only one.

The question of the approach to be taken to these psalms as prolegomena is crucial. They will be read and considered in their genre as Scripture. This methodological recognition of their identity in the Book of Psalms has important implications that can only be admitted and not argued here. They will not be read under the exclusive constraints of their generic identification in form-critical and cult-functional research as "royal psalms," that is, as texts composed for use in various agenda of rituals for reigning kings of Judah. Their relation to a royal ideology of kingship evident in extrabiblical texts from the general culture of the Ancient Near East and their place in the history of religion will not guide the construal. These approaches are valid and have made important contributions to the general understanding of these psalms. In their transmission and shaping and collection as items in the Book of Psalms, they with all the other poetry of the Psalms "ascended" into another genre. They became Scripture, texts whose hermeneutical context is the literary scope of the book in which they stand and the other books of Israel's Scriptures. It is in this identity that they "worked" in relation to Jesus and the community in which the New Testament was written. For the purposes of Christology, it is permissible and appropriate to consider them in that identity.

The interest here is to describe some features of the "vision" in these psalms of YHWH's relation to the "Christ" who speaks and is spoken about in them. The argument is that this vision of the Messiah is as such important material for the work of Christology. The focus will not be on titles and their development in the history of tradition, or their influence and effect on the historical Jesus or the early Christian communities, the frequent procedure in New Testament Christologies. The procedure will be to begin with Psalm 2 in its introductory role and fill out the "vision" of the Messiah from some other psalms whose explicit subject is the Messiah. The exegesis will endeavor to be descriptive, eliciting only what is there in the text, but it will be admittedly selective, guided by the interest of Christology and open on the potential in the language of the text rather than reductionistic.

III. PSALM 2

Psalm 2 is the second panel of the introduction to the Book of Psalms. It is united to the first psalm by the inclusion of 'ashre-sayings ("Blessed," or "How happy") which open the first and conclude the second, and by the repetition of themes from the first (1:6) in the second (2:12). Together Psalms 1 and 2 introduce major topics and terms that are woven through the texture of the entire book. The piety represented by these psalms is beset by the problems of the wicked and the nations. The reader is asked to take both psalms as the voice of the speaker, who identifies himself in 2:7 by an identity given him by God. "The son" pronounces the beatitude of Psalm 1 about the wicked and the righteous and discloses the policy of heaven concerning the nations in Psalm 2.

Psalm 2 deals with the problem of the nations governed by kings and rulers. The autonomous exercise of governance by rulers is portrayed as opposition to the sovereignty of YHWH and his Messiah. The opposition is not related to any particular historical occasion by the text; it is described as a general circumstance and problem for the sovereignty of YHWH.

The idiom of the psalm is that of kingship, the idiom that is central for the theological vision of the entire book. YHWH is the universal sovereign throned in the heavens. Any institution of power on earth that does not recognize that sovereignty disrupts and disturbs the reality of the world.

The strategy of YHWH's rule in answer to the rebellious stratagems of earthly power is the presentation of a king who belongs to the divine sovereignty and represents it. The person and office of this king is wholly the work of YHWH. He is identified by YHWH as "my son," an identity that is the result of a divine "begetting" on the day of his presentation. The implication of the text is that this begetting happens through the divine word, "You are my son." This king is located by YHWH on Zion, the place in the world made holy by the choice of YHWH. The king belongs to the sphere in worldly space where YHWH wills to be present as sovereign; he is inseparably related to the presence of the reign of God in the world.

This king is the person to whom God gives the offer and promise to make the nations of the entire world his *nahlah,* his "assigned portion." In the context of the entire Old Testament, the promise is astonishing in its singularity. Israel and its land are called the *nahlah* of the LORD as the portion in the world acquired by God's salvation history (e.g., Ps. 28:9; 68:9). Rule over the nations is obviously his to bestow, but "the ends of the earth" are never said to be the *nahlah* of YHWH. The nations are to be brought into the reign of God by the Son of God. His rule must correspond to heaven's right and authority. The Messiah will be given power to overcome and claim the powers of earthly rule. But he must ask. His will must be joined to heaven's sovereign will. He must consent to the vocation that sets him in conflict with the rebellious powers of earth for the sake of the reign of God. He must be the Messiah-King-Son in reliance on his identity with the reign of God and the promise of God. From these alone come his power in the world.

In and on the basis of this identity the Messiah calls the kings and rulers of earth to become servants of the reign of YHWH. He teaches the nations the fear of the Lord just as he teaches people obedience to the Torah of the Lord (in Psalm 1). To both he offers a better way than the way that offends the divine sovereignty.

The setting of the self-presentation is the sovereignty of YHWH. The Messiah is identified and described in terms of correspondence to and coherence with the character of the reign of God. It is precisely these dimensions of correspondence and coherence which offer materials for reflection in the work of Christology. These dimensions are what must be looked for in the other psalms that deal with the Messiah.

IV. PSALM 3

Psalm 3 does not mention the Messiah, but before going on to psalms that do, it is important to observe a line of reflection opened by its place as the first psalm following the introduction to the book. The superscription of Psalm 3 names the speaker of the introduction, the David of the books of Samuel. We are reminded of the strange and bitter irony that the king identified as son of God once had to flee from Absalom, his own son. Moreover, he was surrounded by many who said there was no salvation for him in God, an even higher irony. He prays for the salvation of God. God's salvation is foundational for his relation to God. The blessing of the people of God depends on and is given through his salvation. The Messiah in the Psalms and in the Old Testament is a quite human figure, vulnerable to the hostility of his own family and the multitudes. His way is the way of prayer and trust. The third psalm opens up a line of reflection that is a counterpart to the psalms about the Messiah.

V. PSALM 18

Psalm 18 is a psalm of praise for the steadfast love of the Lord manifest in saving help given to the Lord's Messiah, to David and his seed. It is a substantive sequel to the introduction in Psalms 1-2 and 3, because it testifies that the Messiah who holds to the Torah of the Lord and is promised rule over the nation is vindicated in person and vocation when he cries out for the Lord's salvation.

The Messiah, this psalm says, was in the power of his enemies. Their threat was more than mere human hostility. They were instruments of death and Sheol, the elemental powers of opposition to YHWH as sovereign of the universe who brought forth the world out of chaos and life out of no life (vv. 4-5). The salvation of the Lord corresponds to the threat. The Lord intervened as the Most High, appearing in the theophany that clothed YHWH's action against the powers that challenged the divine rule. Cosmic issues were at stake in the Messiah's predicament (vv. 7-15). The salvation of the Messiah is described as the vindication of the reign of God.

The salvation is a vindication of the Messiah, a revelation of God's "delight" in his king (v. 19). The subject of the divine delight is a coherence between the way of the Messiah and the way of the Lord. Both are "perfect" in their ways (vv. 23-30; the Hebrew word is *tamim*, translated "blameless" in v. 23 and "perfect" in v. 30 by NRSV). The Messiah has been perfect in the righteousness of holding to the ways of the Lord known through the Lord's ordinances and statutes. He has been obedient to the will of the divine sovereignty (vv. 20-24). The Lord is perfect in the consistency of his rule and the correspondence between what he promises and does (vv. 25-30). In the salvation of the Messiah, the "perfection" of the faithfulness of the Messiah and the faithfulness of God is known.

It is through the salvation of the Lord that the office and promise of Psalm 2: 8-9 is fulfilled. The predicament of the Messiah when he was in the toils of death and cried out to the Lord was answered by a deliverance that established the Messiah as "head of the nation," and brought a people unknown to him into his service (vv. 31-45). The victory given the Messiah in God's salvation brings about the kingdom of God. Hearing about the Messiah as the vindicated of YHWH compels even foreigners to acknowledge the power of God at work for and in him. God's strength makes the Messiah's way "perfect"

(v. 32, again *tamim,* "safe" in NRSV) because it achieves a coherence between his vocation and his work.

The superscription of Psalm 18 and its other literary context at 2 Samuel 22 connect it with all David's escapes from Saul and all his battles with the enemies of Israel. The psalm stands in that connection as a theological interpretation of David's career as servant of the Lord. There was, says the superscription, "a day when the Lord had delivered him from the hand of all his enemies." Deliverance from all enemies is an eschatological hope of the people of God. This hope was realized one day in David's career as a proleptic manifestation of what God intends to accomplish through David's seed for the servants of the Lord.

VI. PSALM 72

Psalm 72 is a prayer for the king. From beginning to end the psalm is intercession on the king's behalf. The agenda of the intercession covers all the endowments and accomplishments that belong to the royal rule in its fullness and perfection. As the prayer proceeds through its agenda, it becomes apparent that what God is asked to enable the king to do is that which the Psalms elsewhere attribute to the work of the divine sovereignty. The king himself is to be the medium and source of righteousness, well-being (*shalom*), victory, and abundance. He is to exercise universal rule over all kings and nations. His name should endure forever, and the nations bless themselves by that name as God's promise to Abraham is kept through him (compare v. 17 and Gen. 12:13). Especially, the king is to be the officer of the Lord's merciful justice that saves the lives of the lowly and helpless when they cry to him (vv. 2, 4, 12-14). The correlation between the role and the way of the LORD and that of the king for whom the prayer is made is unmistakable. The prayer envisions and prays for a king who will make it possible for the people of God and the nations of the world to live in the kingdom of God. This, the prayer confesses, all depends upon the promise and power of the divine judgments and righteousness in the person of the king.

The prayer is made, says its opening line, for a king who is a king's son. The superscription connects the prayer with Solomon, and the colophon at the conclusion (v. 20) says the psalm is the last in the sequence of David's prayers before the psalms of Asaph begin. Superscription and colophon taken together ask that the prayer be read as David's intercession for his seed and successor, a prayer that the vocation of God's king be realized in his son. In the light of the story of Solomon, it is evident how incompletely the vocation materialized in him. The prayer has a dimension and reach that transcend Solomon and all the kings of Judah. Within the Old Testament, it prays for what is not yet a king whose person and practice bring the people of God and the nations of the earth into the time of the reign of God.

VII. PSALM 89

Psalm 89 is a lament over the rejected Messiah. It is the opposite of Psalm 18 and the contradiction of Psalm 2. It sets forth in anguish an unbearable, inscrutable mystery. The Messiah suffers the wrath of his father and his God, the rock of his salvation. The chosen one is now the rejected one. That reversal is the plot of the psalm and the problem for which it sees no resolution. In its long course, it elaborates more fully than anywhere else the correspondence and coherence between the sovereignty of God and the person of the Messiah, because the theological fact of that relationship is the burden of its dilemma. The theme of the lament is God's sworn covenant to establish the rule of David's house forever (vv. 3-4, 28-29, 36-37). The fate of the Messiah has rendered the steadfast love and faithfulness of God invisible.

The Lord reigns supreme in the heavens, incomparable among all the heavenly powers, who only form the council of holy ones around the heavenly throne (w. 6-8). Correspondingly, according to God's promise, God's king is to be the highest of all the kings of earth (v. 27). The Lord is the cosmic warrior who defeated the powers of chaos and founded the earth and all that is in it (vv. 9-12). The Messiah is a warrior chosen from among the people of God and given power over the unruly forces of history. "Seas and river," the symbols of chaos, will be ordered by his rule (vv. 19-25). Just as the Lord has firmly established his rule over the universe forever, he will establish forever the rule of the Messiah (vv. 2, 28-29).

The point of this carefully drawn parallel between the kingship of God and that of David claims that the latter is integral to the former. The Messiah's rule actualizes in the world what is reality in heaven and cosmos. David's kingship is the agency through which the Lord's rule is extended from heaven to earth, and the divine dominion over cosmic chaos expanded to include historical disorder. Just as sun and moon are in the heaven, so David's line will be the enduring witness on earth to the reign of the Lord.

The time of the psalm, the "but now" of verse 38, is a time for the people of God that stands in utter contradiction to the sworn covenant with David. The defeat, humiliation, deposition, and even death (possibly the inference of v. 45) of YHWH's anointed constitute God's renunciation of the covenant. Divine wrath inexplicably prevails. The steadfast love of God and the righteousness of God are put in question. If the earthly correspondent to the heavenly rule is vanquished and vanishes, what of the heavenly rule itself? That is the overwhelming enigma for which the psalm knows no resolution.

VIII. PSALM 110

Psalm 89, with its shattering quandary, concludes book three of the Psalter. It would seem to set closure on the vision of the anointed king of God and the question of his relation to God. But twice more a voice is heard filling out the vision and addressing the question. In Psalm 110 the voice is that of the Lord, apparently speaking through a prophet. The king is invited to sit on the right hand of the Lord, the place closest to a monarch, the place that identifies a regent with the one whose rule he shares and serves. Another sworn promise of God is given the regent. He is made a priest according to the order of Melchizedek—forever. The Messiah is to be a king whose rule provides a priestly ministry. God himself will be at the right hand of the regent on his right hand, and will establish his reign. His people will respond willingly. The horizon of the psalm is the time when the divine warrior has finally and completely defeated and subjected all the hostile powers of earth to the Messiah, and the promise of Psalm 2 is kept. Until that time the Messiah is at God's right hand, exercising the priesthood of one whose rule mediates between the world and its sovereign. The horizon of the session at the right hand and the royal priesthood is the horizon of history.

IX. PSALM 132

In Psalm 132, the voice is the voice of pilgrims going up to Zion. They speak about the relation between David and Zion and the Lord and hope. The psalm begins as a prayer (vv. 1-10) and concludes with a recitation of the promises of the Lord (vv. 11-18). The psalm beseeches the Lord to remember all the afflictions of David which he endured in finding a dwelling place for the Lord. The establishment of Jerusalem as Zion, the place of the Lord's presence, is viewed as the climax and destiny of David's life. All his troubles were self-denials (vv. 3-5) to provide the place of the Presence, where priests are clothed in righteousness and the faithful shout with joy. The pilgrims appeal to the Lord to be present at the place for the sake of David, his Messiah, whose suffering was the human means of its establishment.

The prayer is grounded in the citation of two divine decrees. The first is the Lord's sworn and certain oath that David's kingship would continue in his descendants, if they keep the requirements of the covenant. The prayer looks for a Messiah whose career is covenant true. The Messiah must actualize the obedience and faithfulness required by the divine sovereignty of the people of the Lord. The second is the Lord's election of Zion as the place of his salvific presence. The afflictions of David served and fulfilled the divine purpose. Place and person are united by the confluence of divine will and human service. Because the two are inseparable in the Lord's reign over earth, the Lord will there bring forth "a horn for David, a lamp for my messiah." The place and the person presented in Psalm 2 as the institution of heaven's reign in the world are here the subjects of hope.

X. CONCLUSION

These then are some of the principal features of the vision of the relation between the Messiah and God in the Psalms. It is of course an Old Testament vision. It is articulated in the vocabulary of its time and in the idiom of the protagonists in which it was given human expression. But its royal, political, military language is not irrelevant as long as the great metaphor of the reign of God is useful to the thinking of faith seeking understanding. The language is not abandoned in the New Testament, but rather redefined and informed by the subject that becomes its content there. The New Testament points to another dimension of the Psalms that is only mentioned in this review because of its concentration on texts that deal with the anointed king of God. That other dimension appears in the sequence initiated by Psalm 3 and comes to fullest expression in Psalms 22, 31, and 69. It portrays one whose forsakenness and deliverance become mysteriously the ground of faith in the reign of God. But that is all subject of another paper.

It serves the purpose of the vision best if a systematic and conceptual condensation is not attempted as a conclusion. Such an abstraction easily becomes itself the subject of thought. The vision is best considered in attempted descriptions that are responses to particular texts and their literary and canonical connections. The vision is never fully in focus, never complete in some logical form. In each text it is a refraction of what the text speaks about.

The vision brings perspective and depth to the New Testament witness to Jesus. When Jesus comes into Galilee announcing that the kingdom of God has drawn near because he is there (Mark 1:15), the vision is in the background. When Jesus at the end of Matthew's Gospel tells his disciples, "All authority in heaven and on earth has been given to me. Go therefore, make disciples of the nations" (Matt. 28:16-20), the vision is in the background. When Paul writes the Corinthian church about the end when Christ hands over the kingdom to God the Father after he has destroyed every ruler and authority and power (1 Cor. 15:24), the vision is in the background. The contribution of the vision to Christology is the perspective and depth disclosed when connections like these are made. In their light, is it to claim too much if we confess that the reign of God was "incarnate" in Jesus?

NOTES

1. The title comes from a significant location, Psalm 89:19.
2. *The Nature and Destiny of Man.* Vol II (New York: Charles Scribner's Son, 1946) 15.
3. *Jesus, God and Man* (Philadelphia: Westminster Press, 1977) 32.

CHRISTOLOGY AND INCARNATION: FULFILLMENT AND RADICAL REINTERPRETATION OF THE OLD TESTAMENT PROPHETS

RALPH W. KLEIN

In Judaism and in Christianity the term *messiah* refers to a "divinely appointed deliverer figure." But while the Hebrew word *mšyḥ*; occurs some 39 times in the Old Testament, it is never used to designate this coming deliverer figure. But make no mistake: there clearly was a hope for a divinely appointed deliverer figure in the Old Testament period and in the last two centuries before the appearance of Jesus, despite the late appearance of the technical term *messiah*.[1]

The theological basis for the messianic hope is the oracle of Yahweh to David, mediated through Nathan, in which God promised: "Your house and your kingdom shall be made sure forever before me; your throne shall be established forever" (2 Sam 7:16). Kingship was not the earliest form of governance in Israel, and there are many indications that it was opposed by many on political, economic, and theological grounds.[2] Nathan's oracle, however, offered theological support for David's kingship and indeed for his dynastic pretensions.

The prophets maintained a constant state of tension with their contemporaneous kings. Isaiah had no use for Ahaz, Jeremiah could not stand Jehoiakim and Zedekiah, and Ezekiel seems to have found few redeemable social values in any of the Judean kings. And yet some of the prophets saw on the other side of their contemporary kings, yes, even on the other side of the demise of the whole Davidic line, a possibility for Yahweh to remain true to his promise to David in changed circumstances. God's kingdom would be exercised through a new king or a new line of kings.

My assignment is to review the passages in the prophets dealing with this hope, to note the differences between this hope and its New Testament fulfillment, and to ponder briefly the term "incarnation" from the perspective of Old Testament studies. All of this is written with the intention and the hope that what we say and do at this Symposium will enhance the life of the whole church.

I. THE MESSIAH IN THE PROPHETS

Messianic passages are conspicuously absent from Hosea,[3] Joel, Amos,[4] Obadiah, Jonah, Nahum, Habakkuk, Zephaniah, and Malachi.[5] In Second Isaiah, the promises made to the Davidic dynasty are "democratized" and reapplied to the people as a whole, without speaking of a coming, divinely-appointed deliverer figure.[6] The messianic passages in the other prophets, however, amply demonstrate the range and power of this hope within the canon.[7]

A. Isaiah[8]

In Isaiah 9:1-7, the prophet describes the great deliverance that would come to three areas of North Israel that had been turned into Assyrian provinces in the eighth century: "the way of the sea, the land beyond the Jordan, Galilee of the nations." God's theophanic appearance (a great light, v. 2) would break the oppressor's rod (v. 4) and consign the military uniforms of the Assyrian invaders to flames of fire (v. 5). It is the birth of a child in the Davidic house, however, that gives this passage its specific shape. This birth is a sign of the validity of the promised deliverance, while the child himself will exercise his royal authority in a rule marked by peace without end. "Justice and righteousness"—we would say, a concern for social justice—will be the king's everlasting attributes. It is the name of this child, however, that rests in most of our memory banks, thanks to Handel's *Messiah,* and that name is most important for understanding the messianic hope of Israel.

The NRSV translates the name as follows:

> Wonderful Counselor, Mighty God,
> Everlasting Father, Prince of Peace.

If this translation is correct, the coming ruler is given wondrous, almost God-like attributes—each of the words is capitalized in the NRSV. To call this Davidic child "Mighty God" is in clear tension with the rest of the Old Testament, that presupposes the human identity of the king and his children and seems intent on limiting any pretensions to deity. For this reason I favor the alternate translation of JPS:

> The Mighty God is planning grace;
> the Eternal Father, a peaceable ruler.

This name, then, like almost all other biblical names, is a sentence that makes a confession about God: God is planning grace, the Father is planning to send a peaceable ruler. It is this divine initiative that is the really good news in this passage, as the last line of the pericope confirms: "The zeal of the LORD of hosts will accomplish this." The name of the new Davidic prince reminds everyone that the ultimate source of deliverance from the Assyrians is God. In fact, this passage assigns no role to the king in effecting this deliverance. Rather, by his name the messiah points people to God; his rule will be marked by a constant passion for justice.

A series of messianic passages in Isaiah 11 adds to the picture. In vv. 1-5 the prophet notes that the present Davidic line must come to an end (stump, roots), before a new dynasty (shoot, branch) can begin. The king will be the son of Jesse and hence a second David. Most importantly, he will be gifted by the spirit. Charismatic endowment was claimed by both Saul and David, but all subsequent kings owed their status to the fact that their father had been king. No historical king after David is said to have had the spirit. This passage, therefore, foresees the Davidic prince as a return to the original contours of the royal house. His gifts of the spirit equip him for leadership in war (v. 2). The king will also be an exemplary judge, not moved by flattery, who will issue stern words of judgment against the arrogant[9] and the wicked (v. 4). His personal "righteousness" and "faithfulness" will equip him for his judicial role. He will be a partisan for the poor and the meek of the earth (v. 4). Kingship is here envisioned living up to its best intents.

A subsequent paragraph predicts peace between wolf and lamb, cow and bear, nursing child and dangerous asp (11:6-9). These familiar lines suggest a return to the conditions of the garden of Eden and characterize the effects of the messiah's righteous reign. They are also a reminder that the messianic hope of Israel is part of a much wider eschatological tradition.[10] so diverse is Israel's eschatological hope that many biblical books can discuss it in detail without ever mentioning the messiah (cf. Daniel).

B. Micah

The central part of Micah's messianic promise is wellknown:[11]

> But you, O Bethlehem of Ephrathah, who are one of the little clans of Judah, from you shall come forth for me one who is to rule in Israel, whose origin is from of old, from ancient days.[12]

Micah starts the new line of kings from Bethlehem, not Jerusalem, just as Isaiah 11 had returned to the stump of Jesse. David was the youngest member of his family, and Bethlehem was among the smallest clans. Yet neither David's youth or Bethlehem's size could thwart God's decision to make someone again be ruler in Israel. The continuity with the line of David will be preserved even if it is necessary to start the line of kings over from its original home town. Other elements in Micah's promise include the return of exiled members of the people (5:3), the king as the channel of food and sustenance for the people, and the expected security for the people (cf. Jer 23:5-6). The king will be a person of peace (cf. Isa 9 7).[13]

C. Jeremiah

The first messianic passage in Jeremiah appears in 23:5-6:

> The days are surely coming, says the LORD, when I will raise up for David a righteous Branch, and he shall reign as king and deal wisely, and shall execute justice and righteousness in the land. In his days Judah will be saved and Israel will live in safety. And this is the name by which he will be called: "The LORD is our righteousness."

I take these words as a contrast to the puppet King Zedekiah, the last ruler of the

Southern kingdom, who had been elevated to kingship by Nebuchadnezzar. The messiah promised through Jeremiah will be a real king, who will exercise wise leadership. "Legitimate branch"[14] might be a better translation than the NRSV's "righteous Branch." The term "legitimate branch" contains an implicit criticism of Zedekiah's credentials. The promise that this king would execute justice and righteousness repeats a theme we found in Isaiah 9 and 11 and stands in sharp contrast to the injustices presided over by Zedekiah's predecessor Jehoiakim (Jer 22:13-17). Jeremiah foresees a united people (Judah and Israel) free from the invasions and exiles faced by the prophet's contemporaries. Most interesting to me is that the messiah again bears a special name: "The LORD is our righteousness," or, perhaps better: "The LORD is the source of our vindication." Zedekiah's name had originally been Mattaniah; it was changed by the king of Babylon who had put him on the throne. The messiah's name change is the result of divine promise. Like the name in Isaiah 9, it indicates that the messiah's efforts are not an end in themselves, but point to the real source of aid: God's inbreaking efforts.[15]

Within the book of Jeremiah this promise is given a later interpretation in 33:14-16[16]: "The days are surely coming . . . when I will fulfill the promise I made to the house of Israel and the house of Judah" (v. 14). With only minor changes from chapter 23, verse 15 repeats the promise to raise up a branch, who will practice social justice in the land. But verse 16 reflects its later chronological setting by narrowing the geographical scope from Jeremiah's united nation (Judah and Israel) to the much smaller expectations of the post-exilic author: Judah and Jerusalem. The name is not given to the messiah, but to the city: This is the name by which it [the city] will be called: "The LORD is the source of our vindication." As the site of the second temple, which brings benefactions to the people, Jerusalem is given a name which expresses its new importance. One might compare the renaming of the "city" in the last verse of Ezekiel: "Yahweh is there" (48:35), as well as the renaming of Jerusalem as Hephzibah (My delight is in her) in Isaiah 62:4.

D. Ezekiel

Ezekiel was a contemporary of Jeremiah during the early days of the Babylonian exile. The final paragraph in chapter 17 promises that Yahweh will take a sprig from the lofty top of a cedar tree and plant it on the mountains of Israel, where it would sprout branches and bear fruit. The prophet expected a future monarch from the descendants of Jehoiachin, not from the discredited line of Zedekiah. When this sprig would mature and become a noble cedar, it would serve, appropriately, as a roost for all kinds of birds. Thanks to what Yahweh would do for Israel, all the trees of the forest—that is, all the nations—would recognize the deity's ability to raise and lower the status of countries or their rulers.[17]

In chapter 34 Yahweh promises to be the good shepherd in the place of the former faithless shepherd-kings, but he also promises to raise up an ideal earthly counterpart shepherd to rule with him (vv. 23-24). This "prince" would be the servant of Yahweh, and he would rule among (not over) the people. Twice it is said of this messiah that he would be "David." This does not seem to represent a hope for the resurrection or return of the first dynastic ruler. Rather, it expresses the view that the coming king, or series of kings, will form a counterpart or parallel to that great king of Israel's early history.

Ezekiel also cites another divine promise: "And David my servant will be prince forever" (37:25). The line of David had come to a dreary end with its final member, Zedekiah. Ezekiel believed that God would restore the dynasty and keep it forever, just he would keep forever the promise of land, of covenant, and of temple. But Ezekiel also shows that kingship in a renewed Israel would be a limited institution. The messiah is designated by the title "prince" (*nāśî'*) instead of "king" (*melek*) cf. 34::23-24).

The monarch of the coming era is always called "prince" in chapters 40-48 of Ezekiel, a title inherited from ancient Israelite tradition, but suggesting here the limited status of the king after the exile. He will be "prince," not king. A discussion of the prince's property in Ezekiel 45:7-8 indicates that he will be given enough income to meet his needs, but the passage ends with admonitions for him not to expropriate land belonging to the tribes and to avoid all violence (45:9). Ezekiel apparently recognized that the nation Israel could not exist without a king, but he also recognized the ambivalent character of kingship itself. The prince's central function in the restored Israel would be that of chief worshiper, sitting in the east gate, on the days of sabbath and new moon. For Ezekiel the real power that would lead to change comes not from the messiah, but from the presence of God which hallows temple, people, and land.

E. Haggai

Haggai prophesied in 520 and attempted to rekindle interest in completing the rebuilding of the temple. Haggai believed that Yahweh's worldwide rule was about to begin. Yahweh himself would destroy the strength of kingdoms and overthrow the chariots and their riders. Then he would take Zerubbabel, governor of Judah, his servant, and make him like a signet ring on Yahweh's hand.

Zerubbabel would be an implement or sign of Yahweh's reign and not a king of an independent kingdom or a warrior king. He would be the opposite of Jehoiachim, the second last king before the exile, whom Yahweh had vowed to cast off even if he were a signet ring on the divine hand (Jer 22:23-25). As Yahweh's chosen one and his servant, Zerubbabel would be a passive earthly symbol of divine sovereignty and not an active messianic figure. The prophet proposed linkages with the past, but did not spell out future political developments.

F. Zechariah

In Zechariah 3:1-10, the prophet Zechariah confirmed the high priest Joshua's new authority, but he also indicated that there would be an ultimate reversal of the present order: "I am going to bring my servant the Branch" (3: 8).

In 4: 6b-10, someone added a supplement to the vision of the lampstand and the olive trees. This secondary passage promises Yahweh's spirit to Zerubbabel, who will be able to overcome all obstacles and finish the temple. While the original vision itself held that both human officials—Joshua and Zerubbabel—are fundamentally equal in importance (4:1-6a, 11-14), this supplement ascribes superior status to Zerubbabel.

In 6: 9-15 Yahweh commanded Zechariah to crown Joshua the high priest and to deliver an oracle that assured the community that a Davidide would one day be installed as king, and that the dual leadership of the community would work in perfect harmony. Thus Zechariah supported a government led by a priestly officer, but hoped for an eschatological role for a son of David.

II. MESSIANIC HOPE AND NEW TESTAMENT FULFILLMENT

To say anything about the relationship between Old Testament and New Testament is very risky, but we need to note continuities and contrasts.

The mere fact that *christos* became such a preeminent title in the New Testament alerts us to the importance of the survey we have been undertaking. The many New Testament attempts to link Jesus to David, even the term "son of David" itself, is further evidence of this connection. The Old Testament messiah's role as one whose name and activity point to God may serve as correction to those who imply that Christianity is a new religion without significant connection to the Old Testament. Whatever Jesus does as the Christ is finally also meant to remind us all that God's commitment to God's people is firm and sure, as it has been in the past.

I would like to reflect on three areas in which there is tension between the Old Testament prophetic materials and the New Testament fulfillments.

(1) At some level of the New Testament record, Jesus the Christ is confessed to be God. Thomas's "My Lord and my God" can serve as a case in point. However complex the factors were that led to that development, the deity of the messiah is totally lacking in Old Testament texts, at least the way I read them. Small wonder that this Christian doctrine leads to conflict and tension with Judaism. The deity of Christ goes beyond what was predicted for the Messiah in the Old Testament material. One might say that the fulfillment turns out to be greater than the promise.

(2) Equally remarkable is the fact that the messiah in the Old Testament does not suffer, let alone die. The only Jewish document I know of that refers to the death of the messiah is 4 Ezra 7, which announces that the Messiah and all humanity will die after a four hundred year reign on earth. Then the world will be judged, the dead raised, and recompense handed out to righteous and wicked (4 Ezra 7:27-35). This death of the messiah lacks all salvific significance. St. Paul presupposes this absence of death in the inherited tradition dealing with the messiah when he writes: "For Jews demand signs and Greeks desire wisdom, but we proclaim Christ crucified, a stumbling block to Jews and foolishness to Gentiles, but to those who are called, both Jews and Greeks, Christ the power of God and the wisdom of God (1 Cor 1:22-24). Any Christian, and especially those of us in the Western church, know how central the death of Jesus is to our faith. That centrality would not be predictable from the side of the Old Testament.

(3) A third discontinuity lies in the presence or absence of real social, political, economic, or material change in the post New Testament world. Justice, peace, and prosperity, according to the promise, were to be hallmarks of the messianic age. If one broadens the data base and considers Old Testament eschatological texts with no explicit reference to the messiah, one finds an even richer array of promises that seem unfulfilled in the Common Era. Have the eyes of the blind been opened, the ears of the deaf unstopped, have the lame been cured, and the desert transformed (Isa 35:5-7)?

Perhaps three answers can be given to this third discontinuity.

In the gospel accounts, social and material transformations were manifest in the miracles and words of Jesus. When John heard in prison what the Messiah was doing, he asked "Are you the one who is to come, or are we to wait for another?" Jesus replied, "Go and tell John what you hear and see: the blind receive their sight, the lame walk, the lepers are cleansed, the deaf hear, the dead are raised, and the poor have good news brought to them." (Matt 11:2-5).

We have learned to account for this discontinuity between promise and Christian reality with the notion of "already and not yet" and with the distinction between the first and the second coming of Jesus. The miracles and even the resurrection of Jesus are viewed as but the first fruits of what is yet to come.

But a third type of reflection has ethical implications. If the church carries on the work of the messiah and if we, the members, are his representatives on earth, we need to remember that the church has often not brought healing and peace, but instead hatred, persecution, and silent acquiescence to evil. Hence we the members have acted as if we did not recognize in Jesus the messiah. If the deity and death of Jesus make him incredible to some, how much more offensive is the failure of the church to inaugurate his new age.

III. INCARNATION

The Old Testament offers little or no help in explaining *cur deus homo*, why God became a human being. At times we speak more broadly of an incarnational theology which fully accepts all creatures great and small. It would be easy to illustrate this positive attitude toward creation and the created order in many Old Testament passages. But I would like to explore with you one Old Testament passage that speaks of God's immanence and transcendence, even of God's self-contradiction in ways that might enhance our proclamation of the good news by highlighting the radicality of the incarnation itself.

I speak, of course, of Hosea 11:1-11. That passage appears in one of the Matthean formula quotations in a way that is jarring at first. When the holy family returns from the flight into Egypt, Matthew writes: "This was to fulfill what had been spoken by the Lord through the prophet, 'Out of Egypt I have called my son' " (Matt 2:15). This is not the literal meaning of Hosea 11:1, which is not even prophetic of the future, but recalls instead God's elective and adoptive call to Israel the child in the course of the Exodus. This call was followed by Baal and idol worship—which would lead to absurd correlations if one attempted to relate Hosea 11: 2 to the life of Jesus.

Matthew seems to be following an eschatological or typological approach. If all Scripture is written for the end time, and we live in the end time, then all Scripture is about us. The modern focus on determining the historical context in which a passage is to be read is not the only way to read a passage. Alternately, one could propose that Jesus is reliving the history of Israel in the gospel of Matthew, including Israel's slavery in Egypt.

Whichever approach he followed, Matthew was able to mine the text of the Old Testament to enhance his message because he believed that the same God who spoke in Hosea was speaking through the life, ministry, death, and resurrection of Jesus of Nazareth. We share Matthew's belief that the God of Hosea and Matthew is identical, but we would illustrate that sameness by far different hermeneutical strategies.

Hosea describes a parent/child relationship gone bad. Despite tender and generous parental activity—picking them up, healing them, teaching them to walk, lifting infants to cheeks—Israel reacted like a highly rebellious teenager. Yahweh concludes that "My people are bent on turning away from me."

What should be the divine response? "Anger, wrath, and punishment," the doctrine of retribution would say. God struggles with that, agonizes with that. "How can I give you up, Ephraim? How can I hand you over, Israel?" God's heart recoils; God's compassion—not his nose—grows warm. And then God decides not to execute anger; God decides to forgive.

Why? "I am God and no mortal." That is a very radical line. God does not have to follow the rules of the doctrine of retribution, the rules of logic, the rules of human parenting. Hosea said this was because God was God and not a human being. The New Testament takes such radicality a step further: God forgives and does not execute wrath precisely *because* God became a human being.

But Hosea cites a second reason for God's strange behavior: "He is the Holy One in your midst." The biblical term *holy* means something like transcendent, other worldly, Godly. But Hosea notes the deep paradox: God, the wholly other, is in your midst—therefore God decides not to execute his anger and not to destroy. The-Holy-One-in-your-midst became flesh and dwelled among us, John affirmed. Is the miracle here God becoming human, or is it not as well the self-contradictory, paradoxical behavior in which God chooses to forgive, all evidence to the contrary notwithstanding?

Christology and Incarnation are both terms from New Testament studies and from the history of Christian doctrine. What we say about the Christ, however, needs to be shaped by Israel's longing for the one who was to come. The radical fulfillment connected with Christology is understood best when we see how far the fulfillment exceeds the promise, especially in terms of the messiah's deity and his suffering.

Our language about incarnation may depend in part on Greek and Persian myths, gnosticism, and other analogies from the history of religions. It also is informed by the whole biblical faith, which knows that God's righteousness leads him to extraordinary efforts and strategies to maintain God's relationship to us. Hosea said: "God contradicts Godself when he decides not to execute his anger. The Holy One chooses to dwell among us."

For someone steeped in Hosea, is the incarnation really a total surprise?

NOTES

1. For a brief survey of messianism between the testaments, see Ralph W. Klein, "Aspects of Intertestamental Messianism," *Concordia Theological Monthly* 43 (1972) 507-17.

2. Frank Crüsemann, *Der Widerstand gegen das Königtum* WMANT 49 (Neukirchen-Vluyn: Neukirchener Verlag, 1978).

3. A (secondary?) passage in Hos 3:5 promises a return "to Yahweh their God and to David their king," thus predicting the reunification of Israel and the acknowledgement of the Davidic dynasty.

4. A (supplementary?) passage in Amos (9:11-15) promises that God will raise up the booth of David (the dynasty, the temple, the southern kingdom?) that is fallen.

5. Malachi speaks of an eschatological prophet who will convert the hearts of parents and children before the great and terrible day of the Lord comes.

6. Isa 55:3. The Servant Songs, so crucial for understanding the death of Jesus in the New Testament are not messianic in the sense used in this paper. Rather, they outline the servant's stance of steadfast faith in the midst of suffering and rejection. The servant is either the prophet himself, or the people as a whole, or both. Second Isaiah does speak of Cyrus, the great liberator of the exiled Israelites, as "his [Yahweh's] messiah" (45:1), but Cyrus is not a descendant of David or the kind of deliverer figure discussed in the rest of this paper.

7. Many of these passages are judged to be secondary by Old Testament scholars and commentators. I believe that a contrary case can often be maintained, but these issues of dating are

only crucial if one is writing a history of the development of the messianic hope, which is not the subject of this paper.

8. It is not clear whether Immanuel (Isa 7:14) is the son of the wife of King Ahaz, the son of the wife of Isaiah, or the son of other, unnamed women. For this reason we are not including it among the messianic texts. But see Matt 2:23. Isa 32:1-8 can also be considered messianic. Just rule will be accompanied by the removal of handicapping conditions.

9. *'ārîṣ* NRSV earth.

10. Isaiah 11: 10 hails the "root of Jesse" as a signal to the peoples. Like David and Solomon he will exercise a "worldwide" reign.

11. For the difficult problems in Micah 5: 2-6, see the commentators.

12. In Matt 2:6 Bethlehem is called "by no means least among the rulers of Judah."

13. Or "This shall be salvation from Assyria" (Mays) or "And this shall be peace" (Smith). In these alternate understandings Micah refers respectively to the messiah as offering security from attack by Assyria or he refers to a period of peace after Assyria is conquered.

14. The term branch *ṣmḥ* is later employed by Zechariah to describe the messiah (3:8; 6:12).

15. It is possible that this name is Zedekiah written backwards. Compare Zedekiah (*ṣdqyhw*) with the LORD is the source of our vindication (*yhwhṣdqnw*).

16. Jer 33:17-26 speaks of a dynastic succession of kings who will ascend to the throne, and of a corresponding line of Levitical priests to offer sacrifices.

17. Cf. Ralph W. Klein, *Ezekiel. The Prophet and His Message*, (Columbia, South Carolina: University of South Carolina Press, 1988) 117.

An Announcement

North Park Theological Seminary in Chicago, Illinois is pleased to announce that the third Symposium on Theological Interpretation of Scripture will take place October 9-11, 1992. The Symposium will start at 1:30 p.m. on October 9 in Nyvall Hall and will extend through noon on October 11.

The theme of the symposium will be Worship. The following persons have agreed to make presentations:

Avery Dulles, S.J.	*Theology*
Donald E. Gowan	*Old Testament*
Daniel W. Hardy	*History & Theology*
Donald Hustad	*Music*
Ralph Martin	*New Testament*
Larry G. Murphy	*Church History*
Marianne Meye Thompson	*New Testament*
Robert Webber	*Theology*
C. John Weborg	*Worship Leader*
Gerald Wilson	*Old Testament*

Persons interested in attending the sessions should write before September 1, 1991 to:

Dr. Klyne Snodgrass
North Park Theological Seminary
3225 W. Foster Avenue
Chicago, Illinois 60625

Meals may be taken at North Park, and assistance will be provided in finding nearby lodging.

Word Of Promise

The Incarnation in the Old Testament*

BALMER H . KELLY

The Incamation is God's new act. It is the new and surprising word which God spoke to make himself known; it is the new and surprising work of salvation. It is set forth in the New Testament as completely new, and yet for all its novelty, it is filled with the sounds of the past. The prophet had declared, "the Lord God will do nothing, but, He revealeth His counsel unto his servants, the prophets" (Amos 3:7, Jewish Version), to which a New Testament writer answered, "In many and various ways God spoke of old to our fathers by the prophets; but in these last days he has spoken to us by a Son" (Heb I:l-2b). The Old Testament faith is that God speaks his word through the prophets concerning what he will do; the New Testament faith is that God has spoken finally and fully through the Son. But by stating it in close connection with the reference to prophecy, the writer of Hebrews makes it plain that this final word is in some sense the ancient word of prophecy made more sure.

That this is indeed the mode of revelation is nowhere more evident than in relation to the Incarnation. Although this is set forth as new and startling in the New Testament, yet the certainty of its happening, and even something of the character of its happening are included in the word which God spoke "in many and various ways through the prophets." Indeed, it is not at all strange that we should go to the Old Testament to learn the word which God speaks concerning the *fact* of his coming and the *manner* of his coming. This is inevitable procedure, if one takes seriously the way the New Testament itself speaks of Christ. One of the ancient heresies, expressed in certain types of Gnosticism, centered in a denial of the fact of the Incarnation, or at least of its solid reality. It is no accident that in making this denial the exponents of this view, at odds with the New Testament, also found it necessary to give up the Old Testament. It is remarkable, not that they thus disposed of it, for it has always been an embarrassment to heresy, but that they understood so well what the Old Testament is saying, that, in fact, it witnesses most powerfully to the reality of the Incamation. We may be sure that they did not find the

---

* Reprinted by permission of the author and current editor of *Interpretation: A Journal of Bible and Theology*. X (1956) 3-15.

Old Testament concerned with Incarnation only in a developmental way, rather as the third act of a play is presumed when two acts have been played out, a kind of historical or logical resolution. That is true of the Old Testament, but these early interpreters did not have that kind of understanding of the biblical revelation; they were not historians and had no historical methods of interpretation. Rather they seem to have found in some definite way, which we cannot dismiss as mere allegorizing, a clear word of promise that the Incarnation would be, and even of the manner in which it would take place, a word so impressive that it must be silenced if the act of God were to be removed from the realm of real happening. Of course there is no disposition to return to the methods or to the conclusions of the Gnostics. But it would be a healthy development for theology if closer attention were paid to the Old Testament in the realization of the possibility that here is a clear and definite word concerning the "thing the Lord will do." This kind of attention would not be satisfied by looking up "incarnation" in a concordance, or even "virgin birth" as though the Old Testament witness would be expressed in fragmentary texts or ideas. The appropriate method will be an examination of the leading concepts of Old Testament thought, and particularly of those that carry forward with especial force into the New Testament. There are many such dominant ideas, some of them having real bearing on the fact and the mode of the Incarnation. Some of the most important ones may be grouped under the general themes: the fact of creation, or God's relationship to the world and man; the fact of individualization, or the relationship of man to the group, under God; and the fact of representation, or the relationship of God to the group through a man.

I. CREATION

The fact of creation, and the character of creation are primary witnesses to the Incarnation. Creation is God's word that the Incarnation will be, the method of creation is his word as to how it will be. Creation is not conceived of in the biblical account, or in the subsequent references to it throughout the Bible, as simply the evidence that God made the world. The doctrine of creation *begins* here, but it is error, whether of the rigidly literalistic or the equally rigidly liberal kind, to suppose that this is the whole biblical concern. The Old Testament itself does rest in the simple fact that God created the world as, for example in the extrabiblical accounts, the pagan gods fashioned the world. The Old Testament faith, which draws heavily in all its strands on the original story itself, is that God made the world by his *Word*, which is the constant, active revelation—it is not too much to say "revealer"—of what and who he is. Thus the beauty of nature, or whatever of order exists in the firmament, or the very structure of existence, these are viewed and valued not just for themselves, certainly not as the comfortable assurance that there is a God, but rather as the sign of *who* God is. Whatever our own private views about general revelation may be, the fact remains that the Bible treats of such a general revelation, and, indeed, gives it weight and authority. To discard it completely does more than enervate the Old Testament and rob it of its living quality; it also cuts the vital connection between the Old and New Testaments, and silences at least one word that God has spoken concerning his work in Christ.

We cannot, of course, go to the other extreme, and see in the fact of creation a testimony equal to the word in Christ. We are not able to, because creation's word remains throughout a word that needs to be explained and, in a deep sense, to be verbalized.

Some modern poet has spoken of the various elements of creation, and particularly the features of beauty and order as "mute messengers of God." And so they are, but herein is precisely the tragedy, the tragedy of a message that cannot be spoken. Here is a word crystallized in rocks and mountains, in life itself, crying out to be spoken. The unending controversy over the relative worth of general and specific revelation did not come about by chance. It is forced upon us by the facts of the Bible, by the fact of this crystallized word. But it is just this kind of word, made visible in creation, that becomes a most potent witness to the Word that is to be made audible.

But once again, the fact of creation is carried to a deeper level in the Old Testament, and this, in turn, becomes a witness to the Incarnation. Creation is not just a matter of rocks and hills, of starry firmament, and the whole order of nature. Creation is also the faith that life, *this* life, including what we term "history" and also the microscopic span of a man's existence, this is the work and concern of God. The Old Testament is plainly preoccupied with this life, with here-and-now. This is evident in the absence of any clear concept of an afterlife beyond the deliberately shadowy outlines of Sheol. But it is also positively present as the prophets scan history, and the sages human existence, and as both see *this* life as the sphere of God's revealing and redeeming activity. All through the Old Testament we are taught to reverence human existence and, more significantly, to examine and search it for signs of God's presence.

The wisdom sages particularly subject life and its concerns to a kind of minute analysis, searching for meaning; and meaning, of course, for the Hebrew is involved in God's presence and blessing. The experience of Job is a crucial point. Here is a place where perplexities abound, but they arise not out of dogma, but out of experience itself. Where theology has no need to deal with life and its situations it can be entirely and comfortably orthodox. Thus the friends of Job are in error not so much in what they believe as in their refusal to subject that belief to the important test of life, Job's life. The opposite is true of Job. There are many implications to his search, but one of the most important is his relentless insistence that life itself is the arena in which ultimate meanings must either be discovered or at least tested and appropriated. His agony is partly the result of the unbearable pull of two radically opposite facts: the one the fact of creation, the other the unmeaning of his own life, and therefore of all life.

Thus we may say in truth that the friends of Job could never have believed in the Incarnation in the orthodox sense, for their conception of existence left no room for it, in fact, had no need for it. But in Job's case—and he is the hero of faith—the Incarnation is the necessary outcome. His cry "He is not a man as I am" is not in a class with predictive prophecy, but it is a mighty word of promise. It says clearly what the problem is, and it also says *where* the solution is to be found. It will not be found finally in the essentially supernatural, or at least unearthly, unrealistic philosophies of the friends, but in the plane of this life, where the problem itself eventuates. We cannot forget that the Book closes with a theophany, not fully satisfying, but at least the answer to the cry of despair which life itself raises, and pointing in the direction of the true theophany which, from the Old Testament's own leading, we know must be neither in whirlwind nor storm, but in humanity.

For it is in the climactic event of creation that the Old Testament word becomes most directly concerned with Incarnation as fact. It is a simplification, yet true, to say that creation itself testifies to the possibility of the Incarnation, the character of created life to its necessity but it is the creation of man that finally testifies to the Incarnation as fact.

Creation does not stop with a materialized Word of God. As the act of creation proceeds in the biblical account we are made sharply aware that the plan which is thus being unfolded is the plan of a temple, and finally at the center of it there is placed the image of God himself, the man for whom the rest is setting and environment, as the command of God to man makes plain. Here the word of creation is made intimate and personal. The Hebrew concept of *word* is basically that of "revelation," particularly revelation of the speaker's nature and character; it is natural, then, that as the creative word comes to its climactic work, the result should be the very image and likeness of the Speaker himself.

In the search for the content of the imago Dei it is important that we not miss the central fact that whatever it consists of, it is still *image* or *likeness*. Moral perfection, intelligence, life itself, whatever is implied in the image, the important thing is that here, in humanity itself, is God's likeness. And that is more than a fact to be admired or applauded. It becomes, as do most biblical facts, an imperative, a command that is to be followed. If it be true that God in creation is saying, "Here in humanity I have placed my image," he is also saying, "Look !" "Look here, for my full image." Here is the command, and consequently the encouragement to seek the Face like our faces, here in short is the real sign that creation is the first step on which the Incarnation follows as a second. Or, to change the figure, here is the first sounding of the word of which the Incarnation is the final, clear utterance, and which the Incarnation itself makes plain. Here is the witness that the image will finally be seen perfectly, not under the distortions of sin and selfwill, but in clarity and in truth.

The possibility, the necessity, and the fact of the Incarnation are all basic in the fact of creation. This is surely John's meaning in his discourse on the relation of the Incarnate word to creation in the prologue to his Gospel. Here in three separate connections he draws the whole together: "All things were made through him. . . In him was life and the life was the light of men. . . . the Word became flesh and dwelt among us." This One, who is the center of the gospel announcement, is the One to the possibility of whose coming creation has always pointed, whose movements in human life and history gave strong indication that he would come, making man forever restless with human existence, and who is the full union of word and flesh of which Adam is the promise.

Nor is this simply the burden of the prologue to the Fourth Gospel. It is the faith of the entire New Testament. In many ways it is saying the same thing that is affirmed here. The New Testament acceptance of the Incarnation as fact gives meaning to some of the Old Testament's hitherto obscure concepts; it also relieves some of the passion of the Old Testament search. It is sometimes pointed out, for example, as a strange thing that the New Testament does not make as much of nature's beauty and creation's meaning as does the Old. It is quite true that there is nothing in the New like the nature rhapsodies of the Old. In one sense they are not needed, for the New Testament was written by men who already possessed the Psalms as the language of their devotion. But in a deeper sense they are not needed, for the life of Jesus of Nazareth is the fulfillment of what the nature rhapsodies are expressing. The absence of such in the New Testament certainly cannot be taken as encouragement for discarding all general revelation as something outworn and outgrown. The New Testament does not concern itself as joyously with nature as does the Old, but that is primarily because the reality of which such concern is a sign has come. The Psalms sing of the wonders of creation, seeing in them the pledge of God's presence in creation and his control of nature. Jesus *is* God's presence, as his life is the manifestation of God's control, not just over an orderly and harmonious creation, but even, as we now dare to see, over a creation turned rebellious to God's will and distorted by the purpose of the Evil One.

In the same way we find the passionate preoccupation of the Old Testament with this life relieved in the New. With the exception of the Epistle of James the kind of search and affirmation we find in the Wisdom of the Old Testament is completely missing in the New Testament, and even in James the passionate questions are missing. The search is really over. The questions have been answered. And they have been answered, just where the Old Testament faith suspected the answer would be found—that is, in life itself.

There is a kind of condensed version of the biblical view of creation to be found in the combination of three passages: the creation story itself, the 8th Psalm, and the 2nd chapter of Hebrews. The faith itself, as set forth in the creation story, and taken up in man's response in the Psalm, is that man, as created by God, is intended to have dominion over all creation, and to hold all in subjection. Against this faith there continually beat the negations of life itself, its failures, its disasters, its seeming powerlessness. And then comes the New Testament witness which, in a section dealing with the very fact of Incarnation, reaffirms the creation faith, adding, in true realism, that still we see "not yet all things in subjection," but also adding the novel faith of the gospel, that "we see Jesus." The Incarnation is a pledge that what creation intimates, and what man's faith takes up and affirms, is indeed true.

The New Testament not only views the Incarnation as the fulfillment of creation as a whole, but also as the final syllable of the Word spoken at first in the creation of man: "Let us make man in our image." The most prominent use that is made of this in the New Testament, of course, is Paul's extended doctrine of the Second Adam. To treat this fully is beyond the scope of this limited paper, but reference may be made to what is much the same idea in the Mars Hill address. There are many different views of Paul's attempt here, as there are different estimates of his success. A consideration of the general New Testament use of the Old makes it conceivable that the analogy of creation is the argument Paul is following in this Athenian address. The argument moves from the futility of seeking God in the temple, to the necessity of seeing him in the near image, that is the image in humanity, and finally to the announcement of the new image in the Second Adam, Jesus Christ. Here in the center of humanism he attempts the most daring humanism of all, which is to say the biblical humanism, following the command which God himself gives when he creates man in his image.

II. INDIVIDUALIZATION

One of the prominent aspects of Old Testament history is the way in which, rising out of the concern for the group, there comes time and again a strong attention to an individual. The Old Testament never rests content for very long with "man" or with the nation, but always moves toward the sharp concept of *a* man, or *the* man. Too much, in fact, has been made of the Old Testament concern with the group or the nation, so that the impression is sometimes given that it presents the nation in such a strong light that all sense of the individual and his importance is lost, in much the same way as in the modern theories of the superstate. It is true, of course, that in dealing with man God moves in the life of the nation; it is true that individuals share in the corporate responsibility and the corporate blessing of the larger group. But it is also true that the large concerns of the Kingdom of God are most often and most clearly seen in much smaller focus, as, for example, in the life of the family unit, and, supremely, in individuals.

The revelation of God to and through Israel begins in the amazing experience of the nation at Sinai. Here God certainly covenants with the group, and directs the formation of the nation as the fulfillment of his purpose. But a glance at the Book of the Covenant which forms the constitution of this group shows many strongly individual features. God speaks to the people, and he calls them to be a nation under God. But in the fulfillment of that high calling they find their duty expressed in a law which itself is phrased, more often than not, in the uncomfortably singular number. And when the spiritual leaders of this nation later set forth the prior history of the people, interpreted in the light of the Sinai experience, they do so by means of stories of individuals, the patriarchs. Here, in the Genesis story what God says to the nation at Sinai is made clearer and more explicit as its implications are illustrated in the lives of individuals.

How often is this same thing true in the subsequent history of Israel. It is the history of *Israel,* but we cannot read very far in it before we are caught up in the story of success or failure of *individuals.* When we start to tell it again, we usually end as did the author of the Epistle to the Hebrews by calling the roll of men of faith. The charismatic leaders, the judges, the kings, the prophets, the multiple simple individuals, the "I" of the Psalms—these all make up a feature of the Old Testament revelation which must not be overlooked. More, it must be heard, for in its own way this too is a word. The hearing of this word schools us to look for the individual.

This is true also in the general movement of the Old Testament. Whatever of group centering is apparent at the first, it recedes as one moves through the pages of Old Testament history. The nation never disappears, but increasingly the individual who stands, as we shall later see, *for* the nation comes into focus. We cannot miss the intensity of individualization in the Book of Job, where the individual becomes the *lone* individual. And much the same is true of the whole later stage of Old Testament thought as witnessed to by Ezekiel's doctrine of individual responsibility and privilege, Jeremiah's own experience, the individual exhortations of the Wisdom writers. These witnesses point the gaze of the beholder not just to this world and to the plane of this life for the arena of God's revealing activity, but they also, and more sharply point to the individual who stands there, distinct from and yet in some sense *for* the group.

It is no accident that it is in this later stage of thought that the concept of the Son of Man comes to expression. It is not appropriate here to enter the long discussion of the meaning of this figure; it can be said quite simply that, excluding the extracanonical apocalypses there is very little in the Old Testament itself to indicate anything other than that the Son of Man is, as his name implies, an individual who stands in a unique way for all mankind, fulfilling God's purpose, and in harmony with his will. The interchange of the expressions "the saints of the Most High" and "Son of Man" in the Book of Daniel, and Ezekiel's use of the expression, both point in this same way. The Son of Man stands essentially for the realization that what the Old Testament has been pointing to all along must be taken seriously in the accomplishment of God's Kingdom, that is, the high and responsible place of the individual.

It is this individual who stands for the nation, either in its entirety, or in its symbolic remnant. Putting together all of the Old Testament expectation concerning God's revealing and redeeming activity, we have the direct sense of movement from the total group to the consecrated group, and finally to the one individual who stands for both, and gathers both into his obedience, just as, all along, individuals have involved the group either in blessing or in judgment. All of this is true also in the concentrated treatment of the "Servant of the Lord" where, as many commentators have pointed out, there is a fluid concept, moving generally in this same direction from the group through the consecrated group to the individual.

There are no real saints and no real heroes in Israel. How, then, it may appropriately be asked, can such individuals be in any sense the word of the future, the sign of One who was to come, whose character and achievement would be so radically different from theirs? But this is the strange thing about the Old Testament; this is the very feature that becomes most strongly forward-looking. The individuals are not ideal, and they do not become more ideal as we move along through the history, any more than Israel became better as she grew older; but their failures, even monotonously repeated failures, somehow become the assurance of final success. Certainly this happened in the case of the definitely individualized hope of the Messiah. The way in which this hope is caught up and repeated in the devotional literature of the Old Testament suggests that it tended to focus on each successive occupant of the throne of David, but that when the particular individual failed to express the ideal of messianic expectation, either in his person or his work, the hope, instead of flickering out, grew stronger and faced forward once more.

When we turn to the New Testament the individual stands in the center. It is so sharp in its intense focus on the individual that it can hardly be said that anything prepares for it. Here, in the New Testament, is *One*, walking with men and yet always distinct from them, identifying himself fully with the group about him and yet still the unique One. Nothing really prepares for this, and yet it could happen only in Israel, for here we have become accustomed to the idea, if not really prepared for it. He gathers, thus, into himself all the movement of the past, as Son of Man, Adam, prophet by reputation and priest and king by work. When the apostles give announcement of the word of salvation which God has spoken in him they naturally turn to the word of the past. When Stephen and Paul and the rest point to Moses, to Abraham, to Joseph, to David, they are not just saying that these *spoke* a word concerning him, they *are* the word of God concerning him. A person who has never read or known the Old Testament may, of course, know what faith in Christ is. But only one who has read it, following the courses of individual men and women, hearing God speak through them, only this one can begin to understand how much is involved in the sight of a baby in a manger, a man walking a Palestinian road, a single cross hung against the sky.

III. REPRESENTATION

There is at least one more way in which the Incarnation may be viewed as the full sounding of the Word whose "goings forth were from everlasting." That is in connection with the consistent Old Testament feature of representation. By this is meant the fact that God not only, calls individuals, separating them from the group, speaking to and through them, but that through individuals he represents himself to men, and through individuals men are enabled to represent themselves to God.

On the one hand there is the figure of the king in the history of Israel, or, in certain periods, the charismatic figure. All are familiar with the tension that exists in the Old Testament itself between the ideal of a kind of theocratic-democracy and the monarchical system as it actually developed under the pressure of national danger. It is important to note that, although the kingship is viewed with suspicion by the early leaders, and always by certain groups, and is constantly under judgment by the prophets, the fact remains that it is viewed as at least potentially a valid and praiseworthy representation of God's relationship to man.

The Old Testament figure of the king is not at all the same as the modern conception of a monarch. In a far more real sense than is possible for our modern ways of thinking to comprehend, the king is intermediary, a figure who gathers into his own person the totality of the people and the nation, but who above all by virtue of his divine appointment, and the divine grace resting on him through his ordination, stands in the place of God, so that it is even possible to address him in such terms as "Thy throne, O God, is forever and forever!" This is not to say, of course, that the actual occupants of the throne achieved any such exalted position, but their failure to do so is the burden of the indictment the prophets, and generally the people, bring against them. The kingship deteriorates in Israel in proportion to its removal from the ideal of popular representation and divine approval. When popular choice was passed by, as it was after the accession of Solomon, and when the prophetic judgments begin to fall, indicating the removal from grace, then the king has ceased to be what he is meant to be, the representative of God's authority and the response and obedience of the people.

The king did not stand alone in this representative character. He was matched by the priest. In the office of the king the emphasis falls more heavily upon the representation of divine authority than on identity with the people; the opposite is true in the case of the priest, so that the emphasis falls upon his representation of man's need and response. In both offices, however, the dual aspect is always present.

As the king gathers into his person the divine-human relationship, so does the priest. Perhaps the clearest definition of his person and work in Israel is the one given *after* the real nature of the priesthood became clear in its fulfillment in Christ, the definition given in the Epistle to the Hebrews, "for every priest is appointed to act on behalf of men in relation to God." Here the twofold nature of his office is quite clear. In ritual and in manifold symbol, but particularly in sacrifice, the priest gives expression to his identity with the people, his action in their behalf, his representation of their need to God, and of God's grace for them. One has only to look at the figure of the priest in the Old Testament as he goes about his work of sacrifice, of prayer, and even of teaching, to see that here is the visible representation of man before God.

Although the greatest care is taken in the Old Testament to keep the two offices of king and priest apart, they actually collide or overlap time and again. In their similarities, and in the tension between them, they are powerful witnesses to the forthcoming work of salvation. They are that because they express in broken fashion what must be true of God's redeeming activity, that it must involve *both* God and man, that it must be the perfect union of authority and response, of need and grace.

When the apostles made the announcement of the redemption which had been wrought in Christ their words were drawn from the vocabulary of the Old Testament, words like "Messiah," "Son of David," "Servant." And when the proclamation is expanded in the apostolic writings the whole symbolism of the Old Testament is rehearsed as it is seen fulfilled in Jesus Christ. They did not draw upon the Old Testament simply for insight into the Atonement. They did so equally for insight into the Person of the Lord. The repeated reference to the 110th Psalm with its mysterious reference to the "priest forever, after the order of Melchizedek," points to the conviction that already in the Old Testament concept of representative king or priest God is speaking the word he will finally speak in his Son. And if it must be spoken at first in broken fashion, in two figures instead of one, that points all the more surely to the time when it will be one, and to the One in whom authority and service, grace and response can be in perfect union.

One thing more should be said. It is instructive to see the contrast to the Old Testament conceptions in the Intertestamental literature. Here the promise of creation, the importance of the individual, and the fact of representation run out into the dry sands and into silence. Creation is promise, as created man is a forecast of God and man in perfect union. But in the Intertestament thought the real fulfillment is forgotten as man's hopes turned to the repetition of the past. Creation becomes here only the sign that God will restore the world to the state of the garden of Eden. This materializing of the promise of creation was matched by a political interpretation of the individual who represents God and man. The political pretension of the Hasmonean dynasty was an attempt to combine the offices of priest and king, but it was only pretension and it failed, in the end, because it actually represented neither God nor man. Finally, the most tragic development of the whole period was the removal of all sense of representation from the ideally representative figure, the Son of Man. In reaction to distress and to repeated disappointment, the sense of the One who would be *all in One* was lost, or replaced by the expectation of One who, in supernatural splendor, would be the antithesis of man. To this purely, heavenly being the title "Son of Man" clung in pathetic denial of his real character.

And then the Lord came and reaffirmed the word of the past, in his person and in his work. It was as the fact of creation, and especially the fact of the creation of man in the image of God had said it would be—not a God in disguise as a man, but God and man in one, the Second Adam whose birth was, like the first, the union of the clay of humanity with the breath of God, who was, therefore Immanuel, God with us. He came as the word of the past had said he would, the word of the individual not isolate and removed, but so much man himself that even in his resurrected form he could be mistaken for a gardener, or for a stranger along the way. He came, as the word of the past, the word of representation had said he would come—unbelievably king and priest, as one who, holding all things in his hand, stooped to wash the feet of the disciples.

The Old Testament does speak concerning the Incarnation, concerning the fact and concerning the way. What it has to say is important because it leads us to the New Testament, and thus impresses us again with the wonder and glory of God's revelation of himself. But it is far more important just because it is a Word of God, and as such has something direct to say to us. It tells us something we might miss. It tells us that the Incarnation is not to be thought of as a kind of accidental joining of God and man, the human and the divine, but as the fact that God and man are one, or, as the marvellously gracious words of the Epistle to the Hebrews have it, that God "is not ashamed to call [us] brethren." It tells us, moreover, not just what the Incarnation is, but in a real sense why it is. That "why" is rooted in the necessity of man, the man who cries out that God is not a man as he is, the man who has eternity set in his heart and is not able to fill it with the world's experiences. But above all, it is rooted in the nature of God himself, the God who is not man, but who has created man and will not let him go.

The Son Of Man And The Incarnation

I. HOWARD MARSHALL

If Barnabas Lindars is right, this paper could be one of the shortest on record in this Symposium! According to his book on *Jesus Son of Man,* the term "carried no christological meaning as such" on the lips of Jesus.[1] Similarly in one of the most recent contributions to the discussion D. R. A. Hare comments that "Jesus' use of *bar enasha* communicates nothing to us about 'Jesus' own Christology,' except that he regarded modesty in speech as an appropriate form of behavior."[2] These two comments may be sufficiently startling for more traditionally-minded students to make it necessary for us to retrace the route by which their authors have been led to them, and to ask whether perhaps, despite assertions to the contrary, the Son of man is alive and well, and the rumors of his decease have been, as Mark Twain said of his own obituary notice, "greatly exaggerated."

Much previous study of the topic has been largely (and necessarily) centered on exploring the background of the phrase, assessing the authenticity of the sayings in the Gospels using it, and thereby reconstructing something of the thinking of Jesus and of the early church. But the question of the significance of the phrase for Christology, and specifically for the incarnation of the Son of God, has not been explored to the same depth, and it is to this topic that we must turn. Unfortunately, it is impossible to do so without giving some kind of survey of the various positions taken by scholars on the subject of the authenticity and original wording of the sayings.[3]

I. PROBLEMS OF RECONSTRUCTION

Let me try to outline the nature of some of the problems which arise:

A. Synoptic and Johannine Sayings

There are sayings ascribed to Jesus which use this term in the Synoptic Gospels and in the Gospel of John, and, despite some common emphases, there is sufficient difference between them to justify taking John on its own and recognizing that in this area also the teaching of Jesus in John has been refracted through the mind of the Evangelist. The question of Johannine Son of man theology forms an important problem on its own which can scarcely be tackled within the limits of the present paper.[4]

B. Authentic and Inauthentic Sayings: Jesus and the Early Church

Even within the Synoptic Gospels we need to recognize that the final shape and working of the teaching ascribed to Jesus is due to the Evangelists and also reflects the handling of the tradition by early Christians during the period before it was committed to writing in the Gospels. In theory, therefore, we can trace three levels in the transmission of the sayings:

1. What Jesus actually said.
2. What was transmitted orally.
3. What was written down in the Gospels.[5]

Particularly important in the present investigation is the fact that the modification of sayings in transmission may have included the addition or subtraction of the crucial phrase in which we are interested, "the Son of man." Scholars who are sceptical about the originality of the phrase on the lips of Jesus have sometimes concluded, falsely and illogically, that the presence of "the Son of man" in a saying indicated that the saying as a whole was inauthentic.

C. Subject and Predicate

A further distinction is necessary between what the phrase "the Son of man" in itself may signify about Jesus and what is said about him in the saying. Thus if somebody in England says, "King George died in 1952," the use of the term "king" carries a whole set of implications regarding the status and functions of the person thus described, and this aspect of the statement is distinguishable from the statement made about the subject, namely that he died. So too we must distinguish between what may be implicitly said about Jesus in referring to him as the Son of man and what is explicitly said in the remainder of any given saying.

In particular, recognition of this distinction may alert us to the question whether certain kinds of statement about Jesus are associated (whether exclusively or otherwise) with use of the term "the Son of man."

D. Self-Designation and "Title"

In current scholarship the debate about the Son of man has centered on the question whether the phrase as used by Jesus was purely some kind of self-designation or whether it was a means of identifying him as the figure described as "a being like a [son of] man" in Daniel 7.13. (I use this cumbrous form of words in order to avoid the very questionable term 'title'.)

It should be added, however, that some scholars have recently begun to ask whether the common assumption that the Evangelists used the phrase in the latter way, i.e. identifying Jesus as *the* Son of man, is justified; was it merely a way of referring to Jesus based on his own use of it simply as a self-designation?[6]

E. Some Earlier Hypotheses

I am going to shorten the discussion by taking one conclusion for granted. Until about 1975 or so the scene was dominated by two main hypotheses, both from Germany. On the one hand, there was the hypothesis stated by R. Bultmann and developed especially by H. E. Tödt that Jesus used Son of man only in a few sayings and with reference to a coming figure, quite distinct from himself, who would be active at the Last Judgment; the rest of the sayings were due to the church identifying Jesus himself with this separate figure, and then creating further statements about Jesus himself. On the other hand, there was the view taken by P. Vielhauer and developed in his own way by N. Perrin that none of the sayings was authentic in the teaching of Jesus and that the early church created the lot.

These two hypotheses have largely lost support in contemporary discussion, although it is true that many of the sayings whose authenticity created difficulties for scholars in these two groups continue to do so today but for slightly different reasons. I therefore propose to ignore them in this discussion.[7]

F. The Main Critical Issues

We have now cleared the ground sufficiently to examine the question of the use and significance of the term in relation to Christology, and it will be clear that three main problems have emerged:

1. What did Jesus teach or imply about himself in the authentic Son of man texts and what did the early church understand by the Son of man texts?

2. In dealing with the first problem, we need to ask what was taught or implied by the use of the phrase Son of man in the texts and what was taught or implied in the things said about the Son of man in them?

3. Did the phrase Son of man function as a self-designation of Jesus or did it have some kind of "'titular" significance?

We shall find that this third problem is the one that can most fruitfully lead us forward in our discussion, and we shall concentrate attention on how Jesus may have understood his own status and role.

II. "SON OF MAN" AS A SELF-DESIGNATION IN THE TEACHING OF JESUS

In current discussion the issue of what Jesus actually said has crystallized around a linguistic problem. On the one hand, there are a number of sayings in the Gospels where Jesus can be speaking only of himself and does so in a way which rouses echoes of the passage about "[a figure] like a man"—"like a human being" if you wish, but undoubtedly a male figure is envisaged[8]—who is given authority by the Most High in Dan 7. On the other hand, there are sayings where there is no apparent allusion to the figure in Dan 7 and where it has been suspected that Jesus is simply using an Aramaic idiom.

The precise nature of this putative idiom is disputed. According to G. Vermes,[9] *bar^{e}nash(a)* was used out of modesty or in embarrasing circumstances as a means of self-reference to refer to the speaker alone, although the third person nature of the phrase meant that it could be misunderstood. According to P. M. Casey[10] and B. Lindars[11] *barenash(a)* was used in statements about people in general which also applied to the speaker. It could not be used, on this view, to make statements that were *exclusively* true of the speaker. Both of these groups of scholars then claim that Jesus himself used the phrase in this manner, i.e. as an Aramaic idiom.

Both also claim that the character of the phrase meant that it could not be used as a so-called title, i.e. to refer to some kind of person or role with which Jesus could identify himself. There was, in other words, no existing concept of "The Son of man" as a figure with whom Jesus could identify himself. It was the early church which picked up the phrase from its genuine use by Jesus, made the link between it and the phrase in Dan 7, identified Jesus with the figure described there, and then proceeded to elaborate an understanding of him as the Danielic Son of man through the creation of a larger body of sayings which they attributed to him.

A. Casey and Lindars hold that there is a small group (no more than about 12) authentic sayings of Jesus in which he uses *bar^enash(a)* as a means of saying things about himself which are true of him because they are true of "everybody" (where "everybody" signifies "everybody in the appropriate context"). Casey's list includes:

Mark:	Mk	2:10, 28; 8:38; 9:12; 10:45; 14:21a, 21b
Q	Mt	8:20 = Lk. 9:58
		11:19 = 7:34
	Lk	12:8 (diff. Mt. 10:32)
		12:10 (diff. Mt. 12:32
L	Lk 22 48[12]	

B. Vermes argues that there is a group of about 20 saying in which Jesus was using the phrase *bar^enash(a)* to refer only to himself, but because the phrase was in the third person it could have been misunderstood by his audience. This group of sayings includes those in Casey's list (but not Mk 8:38 and Lk 22:48) together with Mk 8:31; 9:9; 10:33; 14:41; Mt 16:13 (diff. Mk 8:31); Lk 11:30 (= Mt 12:40); Lk 19:10; 24:7.[13]

If we now look at the Casey-Lindars sayings in their hypothetical original forms, we find that Jesus says a number of things about himself in such a mode as to avoid "being and sounding unduly arrogant, self-centred or humiliated."[14] They include:

1. People (including me) have authority to forgive sins.
2. People (including me) are masters even of the sabbath.
3. People who speak against anybody else (including me) can be forgiven, but not those who speak against the Holy Spirit.
4. If anybody confesses me before men, people (including me) will confess them before the angels of God (and if anybody denies me . . .).
5. Animals have holes and birds have nests, but people (including me and my followers) have no homes.
6. People (including me) go to their death, as it is written of them .
7. But woe to the person who betrays people (including me).
8. People (including me) will die, and after three days will rise.

9. People (including me) come not to be served but to serve, that is, to give their lives as a ransom for many.

10. Judas, are you betraying people (i.e. me) with a kiss?

The Christological significance of these two views can now be stated:

For Casey and Lindars Jesus is speaking as a typical man, and the term *barenash (a)* characterizes him as such. Nevertheless, in what is said about him in these sayings "he did preach with authority, and with total confidence in the divine authorization of a mission in which he brought the good news of forthcoming salvation.'[15] Similarly, Lindars holds that Jesus uses the phrase to speak of himself ironically. He was primarily concerned for his mission, and he used this curious phrase in order "to make his audience think more deeply about their reactions to him."[16]

It follows that on this view the phrase *barenash(a)* itself says nothing about who Jesus is (other than implying that he is a man like anybody else), but may encourage people to ponder who this person is about whom such things are said.

The situation is not so very different if we take the view of Vermes. In this case, we have much the same set of predicates, but the term *barenash(a)* now refers specifically and only to Jesus, and consequently the sayings have something more like their traditional meaning. In both cases, however, the phrase itself says nothing about Jesus because it is simply a way of making statements about himself.

Nevertheless, it is important to note that for these scholars the predicates of the *barenash(a)* sayings considered so far are taken to be authentic and revelatory of important aspects of Jesus' self-understanding. Here it may be worth quoting Lindars at length:

> The authentic Son of Man sayings reveal Jesus as one who was wholly committed to this vocation. He regarded himself as certainly not less divinely inspired than John the Baptist. (a). Indeed, he repudiated any attempt to deny the divine source of his ministry as nothing less than blasphemy against the Spirit of God. (b). He held that he had a unique task to perform for his own generation, comparable to that of Jonah. (c). This included the gospel of forgiveness of sins. (d). Though the element of grace predominated in his preaching, he also demanded radical renewal, and his requirements of a prospective disciple could be stern. (e). He required his teaching to be put into practice, so that it affected public attitudes; acceptance or rejection of him from this point of view had decisive importance, because it would be the criterion for judgment at the coming of God. (f). When faced with danger to his life, he would not allow that to alter what he conceived to be his duty. (g). He declared that he must fulfil his destiny, whatever happened. (h) He was prepared to risk his life for the salvation of those to whom he had been sent .[17]

This is very positive statement of the implications of the genuine teaching of Jesus. And if the kind of approach taken by Lindars is valid, then it positively invites readers of the Gospels, as it invited the people of Galilee, to consider the implications for themselves and to ask: Who then is this who speaks in such a manner?

The kind of Christology which is to be found here appears to express a self-understanding of Jesus as a prophetic type of person who is committed up to the hilt to his mission, who is prepared to die for it, and who regards the consequences of accepting or rejecting his words as absolutely crucial for his hearers. On this view, however, Jesus does not express anything about his own status, and the term *barenash(a)* does not give us any light on it. Indeed, it could be argued, Jesus speaks with a remarkable modesty and self-effacing spirit. The incarnation, if that is the right term to use, is of a person who is thoroughly human, is conscious of no special relationship to God other than that of having a specific calling to speak with God's authority, and who makes no use of any existing categories to clarify his role.

It may be too soon to come to a definitive evaluation of this proposal, especially as certain aspects of it demand a specialist knowledge of Aramaic which I cannot claim. Suffice it to say that there are a number of critical questions which can be asked and that there is room for continuing debate.

1. A preliminary problem is that on the Casey-Lindars view Jesus is said to use *barenash(a)* to make statements which could be true of anybody and yet somehow these statements are really true only of himself and led his followers to conclude that he had a unique position. So far as Lindars is concerned, the idiomatic usage of *barenash(a)* is sufficiently explained by the considerations of modesty and almost embarrassment already mentioned. But, if this is the case, the suggestion that Jesus spoke in this way to invite consideration of who he was seems rather weakly based. Since, by definition, Jesus was saying things that did not differentiate him from other people, it is hard to see how the *barenash(a)* sayings could have the effect of making people see how he was "different."[18]

2. Again, if Jesus said similar things to these about himself without using *barenash (a)* the case that he uged this idiom to make people ponder about who he was becomes less convincing, and one is bound to ask why he sometimes said things using the idiom and sometimes didn't.[19] The case that he was deliberately maintaining a low profile by using the phrase looks less credible.

3. Athough the *barenash(a)* sayings on this view imply that Jesus said nothing directly about his own status, it is highly unlikely that this question did not arise or that Jesus himself did not raise it. There are passages in the Gospels which indicate that people did ask "Who then is this?" or "By what authority do you do this?" And further light may be shed on this issue by examining the passages where Jesus does speak directly and unambiguously about himself using the first-person form of expression.

If we make a sample probe based on the sayings of Jesus in Mark, we find that Jesus uses the "I-form" in the following categories of sayings:

a. In ordinary every-day speech to refer to himself with reference to "my mother," or to ask, "who touched me? " (Mk 3: 33-5; 5: 30) .

b. In prayer to God (Mk 14: 36) .

c. In some authoritative sayings, "[Amen] I say. . . " (Mk 3:28; et al.).

d. In a series of sayings in which people are called to follow Jesus or to come to him. Here may be included passages about confessing/denying Jesus (Mk 1:17; 2:14; 8:38).

e. In reference to his having come or being sent (Mk 1:38; 2:17).

f. Where he refers to action in his name, or for his sake (Mk 8:35; 9: 39) .

g. With reference to his baptism/cup, where the indirect nature of the reference may be sufficiently safeguarded by the metaphor (Mk 10:39).

h. At the Last Supper, where he is with his disciples only. Note 14:28 where he will go before them to Galilee (Mk 14:28).

i. In self-identification using "I am" (6:50; 14:62).

This list is incomplete, and it is admitted that not all the statements may be authentic as they stand. But it is clear that, apart from fairly normal uses, there is a set of sayings in which Jesus issues authoritative commands, and a series relating specifically to following him in discipleship. In these ways Jesus presents himself as an authoritative figure.

The important point which emerges is that Jesus can and does speak with authority about his own role as the leader of the disciples. This suggests that the rather minimalist Christology found by Lindars does not square with the rest of the evidence. It also suggests that the case that Jesus did not assert his authority openly or speak about himself openly and directly is not sound.

4. An analysis of the sayings suggests that the Casey-Lindars type of explanation may work for some of them, but it raises considerable difficulties. In fact, half of Casey's examples do not work satisfactorily. None of them demand his explanation, although for one or two (2., 3., 10) it is not altogether impossible.[20]

Faced by the fact that the alleged Aramaic idiom does not work satisfactorily for the sayings in the Gospels, we are bound to ask whether the usage of the idiom has been correctly identified. Here it seems to me that a better explanation of this group of sayings is that pioneered by Vermes and now upheld by D. R. A. Hare who hold that Jesus used an Aramaic phrase as a self-designation to say things that were true of himself and not necessarily of other people—just as a child might say with respect to herself "This little girl is hungry."[21]

If we now consider the same group of sayings in the light of the explanation that *barenash(a)* refers only to Jesus himself, then the situation is different. There is no difficulty about understanding the sayings in this way. In every case Jesus can be making a statement that is true of himself specifically.[22] The predicates do not need to be forced into unnatural meanings but can be understood straightforwardly as statements about Jesus himself. However, for these scholars the phrase itself still says nothing of Christological significance. Whether it has such significance can be deternined only when we bring in the rest of the evidence. There remain a number of Son of man sayings which have so far been excluded from reference because, it is argued, they do not fit in with the assumed Aramaic idiom, and therefore must represent creations or adaptations by the early church.

III. SAYINGS WHICH MAY HAVE A "TITULAR" CONTENT

We must now reconsider these sayings. We have to bracket off a number of cases where Son of man (or its equivalent) can plausibly be regarded as editorial or as coming in at the stage of tradition.[23] This leaves us with the following to be investigated:

Mark	Mk 8:38; 13;26; 14:62
Q	Mt 24:27, 37, 39, 44 = Lk 17:24, 26; 30 and 12:40
	Lk 6:22 (diff. Mt 5:11)
	Lk 12:8 (diff. Mt 10:32-3)
M	Mt 10:23; 13:37, 41; 19:28?; 25:31
L	Lk 17:22; 18:8; 19:10; 21:36

Most of these sayings fall into the category of future references, and they cannot in general be regarded as examples of the postulated "generic" Aramaic idiom used in appropriate circumstances, since they make statements true only of one specific *barenash(a)* Further, if the character of the phrase *barenash(a)* is such that it cannot be used as a title or means of reference to an existing concept, then occurrences in the Gospels which have this character cannot be authentic as sayings of Jesus originally uttered in Aramaic. It follows that such allusions were created in the Greek-speaking church.

What are we to make of them?

A. Mark

Mk 13:26 is clearly a quotation from Dan 7:13f. and implies that this passage, understood to be prophetic, will be fulfilled at the end of the age by the coming of the Son of man to gather his chosen people. Later in the chapter it is probably the same figure who is referred to as the master of the house who will come to his servants. Further, earlier in the chapter there is reference to the coming of the Messiah, and it is improbable that two different figures are expected to come. Here, then, we have a clear understanding, supported by the context, of the Son of man as the Danielic figure.

Similarly, in 14:62 the contextual indicators make a Danielic allusion unmistakable.

This leaves the problem of Mk 8:38. Here the reference is future and the contextual indicator is "when he comes in the glory of his Father with the holy angel." This could awaken an echo of Daniel 7 in the reference to the holy [angels]. The saying is odd in that it refers to "his Father." This difficulty is eased if Son of man is a self-reference so that "his Father" signifies "my Father" which is a typical manner of speaking by Jesus. The oddity of the language may be due to the fact that Jesus does not speak directly of coming himself in the future.

B. Q

In the Q material, the future references are generally thought to be more original in their Lucan wording. In Lk 12:40 the parable of the waiting servants is explained in terms of the coming of the Son of man. (Just as in Mk 13). In the narrative setting of Lk the disciples know that the Son of man will function at the last judgment. The new element is the coming. In Lk 17 the Son of man has his "day'" when he is revealed, and there is also reference to his "days." It seems to be assumed that people know that he is coming, and the question of what then happens is the issue. His coming is associated with judgment.

In the Marcan material, as we have seen, there are contextual indicators that Daniel 7 is in mind. These are not so conspicuous in the Q material, but it could be argued that references to the future activity of the *barenash(a)* would necessarily be taken as having a background in Daniel 7, or in traditions based on it. It has, of course, been argued that *barenash(a)* was a general term and could not be used specifically to mean "that man" —pointing the hearers/readers to a particular, known figure, but I am not persuaded that the case has been made out.[24]

C. Special Matthew

Mt 10:23 likewise takes for granted that people know what the coming of the Son of man is; it is used as a known event to indicate that the disciples will not get round all the cities of Israel in the time available (rather than to say that he will not come until they have got round them all).

In Mt 13:37 the Son of man sows the good seed in the world, and the reference could be simply to Jesus himself. In 13:41 the time is the end of the age when the Son of man sends his angels to get rid of evildoers—a negative counterpart to the gathering of the elect. So 13:41 links most closely to Mk 13:26.

In 25:.31 there is a judgment scene. The Son of man comes in glory, with his angels, and sits on his throne and judges. He is identified as the king. All this appears Danielic and causes no serious problems. In 19:28 there is an almost identical reference to the Son of man sitting on his throne and to judgment shared by the Twelve. The clause looks like a Matthaean addition to clarify the passage and to make it clear that Jesus is not excluded from the judging process. Both passages may presuppose the link with Ps 110:1 which appears explicitly in Mk 14:62.

D. Special Luke

Turning now to Luke, we note 6:22, which may simply be a self-reference (it cannot be generic). 17:22 talks about desiring to see one of the days of the Son of man, and may be modelled on 17:26. But the highly unusual phraseology speaks rather against Lucan creation. 18:8 assumes that the Son of man will come and asks whether he will (still) find faith when he comes. 19:10 is in the Zacchaeus story and need be no more than a self-reference. 21:36 is the conclusion of the apocalyptic discourse in its Lucan version and refers to people surviving every temptation to stand at last before the Son of man. 22:48 we have already considered. 24:7 is a reference to the passion predictions and may be a Lucan summary of them. 17:25 should not be overlooked; it carries on the Son of man saying in 17:24 and indicates that the coming Son of man is the Son of man who suffered and was rejected.

Summing up the point made in these texts we have:

1. There are unmistakable references to Dan 7 in Mk 13:26 and 14:62.

2. There are probable allusions to Dan 7 when we hear of glory, angels coming (possibly, being revealed), judgment. The coming is spoken of as something taken for granted that needs no explanation, and this suggests that the speaker/writer assumes that the audience recognise the allusion to Dan 7.

3. There is the gathering of the elect, which raises echoes of 1 Enoch.

4. The Son of man has a day. This may be a development of the idea of the day of Yahweh. It is not based on Dan 7.

The question now is whether this teaching is credible and even probable on the lips of Jesus. Is there a continuum with the sayings which we have already examined? And is there an implicit significance derived from apocalyptic?

1. There is no reason why Jesus could not use *barenash(a)* as a self-designation to

refer to his future role—if it had become an established usage on his part and if it is granted that it could be used purely to refer to himself rather than to make generic statements.[25]

2. If so, it also seems likely that he could use it to imply a fulfilment of Dan 7 in himself. Dunn argues that he did do something like this, that he saw the coincidence between his use *barenash(a)* and the occurrence of this phrase in Dan 7 and then proceeded to incorporate allusions in his teaching.[26]

3. Further consideration needs to be given to whether Jesus developed the concept of his own future role as the *barenash(a)* primarily from reflection on Dan 7 or from the consciousness that other roles were being devolved on him by the Father. It may be that it was the future coming of the Lord on the Day of the Lord for judgment which was transferred to Jesus, and that it was then in the light of this consciousness that the link between Jesus and the role of the Son of man in Dan 7 was developed or strengthened.

What is clear is that if we start from Mk 13:26 and 14:62, then plainly the hearers/readers could have recognized that Dan 7 was being quoted and that therefore in speaking of a person who will come on the clouds Jesus was identifying himself as the *barenash(a)* with the Son of man in Dan 7. It was surely quite simple for a Jewish reader to make this link.

We can thus come to the view that one important factor which led Jesus to see his role in terms of Dan 7 was by reason of what he believed that he was going to do, rather than primarily because he knew himself to be the Son of man.[27] If there is anything in this hypothesis, then it makes it easier to understand how Jesus could move from a self-designation to a more technical use of the phrase.

The immediate implication of this teaching is that Jesus claims for himself a significant eschatological role which has important consequences for his self-understanding. If it is correct to hold that he saw himself in this way, then clearly this has implications for the self-understanding expressed in the earlier group of Son of man sayings, and it can be discussed whether they do not implicitly contain the concept of a figure destined to wield authority who is currently humiliated and rejected and whose authority is not accepted.[28] But it also becomes necessary to ask whether the term "Son of man" in these sayings, as opposed to what is said about his future role, carries implications which are important for christology.

IV. THE SON OF MAN TRADITION?

We therefore need to explore the significance of the Son of man in Daniel and in Jewish understanding of that figure.

A. Solidarity with the Human Race and Israel

First, there is the significance of the human character of the figure. An older view was that the Son of man is essentially a human figure. A phrase which could simply refer in Hebrew to a member of the human race came to be used on occasion in contexts of weakness and frailty and even of human mortality (Ps 8; Ezek). Thus the term itself could come to have such associations, and in Ezekiel the translation "mortal man is found in some English versions. (From this starting point it has often been thought to express the humanity of Jesus, his solidarity with the human race rather than his divinity.[29]) This understanding could be present in Dan 7 where the human figure stands in contrast with the animals symbolizing the great empires.

This point has been developed to some extent by M. D. Hooker.[30] She finds a tendency in Jewish literature to identify Israel with man. Thus there would be a close link between Jesus as the Son of man and Israel, and the term would stress his solidarity with Israel.

B. Canaanite Mythology

A number of scholars have argued that the imagery reflects some existing mythology, and have held that an existing myth of a person who receives authority from God is here used as a symbol for Israel. An elaborate form of this view was developed by C. Colpe,[31] based ultimately on the myth of a younger god being brought to the Ancient of Days and receiving power from him. The human character of the figure may reflect a dim myth of Adam as the first man who receives authority from God over creation.

The existence of such mythology makes this view seem plausible.

C. A Purely Symbolic Figure

Against this hypothesis we have the claim of M. Casey that the Son of man in Daniel 7 is purely a symbol for the Saints of the Most High. The Son of man does not do anything and has no experiences; hence there is no "Son of man concept." There is no drawing upon earlier mythology.

D. The Apotheosis of the Son of Man

Another possibility is that the Son of man is a figure who is apotheosized or turned into a divine figure in the vision. Thus M. Black thought that the scene represented the apotheosis of Israel.[32] F. F. Bruce suggests that a figure who is treated as the Son of man by God is being recognized as his Son or equal.[33] The theory that a human figure with divine authority is being portrayed is certainly worth consideration.

E. The Problem of a Messianic Interpretation

Various scholars have suggested that in Dan 7 the Son of man does not represent an individual figure. Dunn comments: "There are no good reasons for the hypothesis that Daniel or his readers would have understood the human figure of his vision as a particular individual."[34] This seems to me to be an extraordinary statement in view of the fact that this is precisely what some readers of Daniel did do. Contemporary Jewish understanding seems to have made the Son of man into a figure of authority, a messianic type of being. The evidence for this lies in subsequent Jewish literature, 4 Ezra and 1 Enoch, where we find two things happening .

First, the term Son of man is not used as a *title* for a being. In 4 Ezra there is reference to a figure like a man who is clearly based on the vision in Daniel 7. This figure is interpreted as a symbol of the Messiah.[35] Casey concludes that this does not provide evidence of a Son of man concept in Judaism. But that is not the point. The important feature is that what is said about the figure in Daniel 7 is made the basis for what is said about the Messiah, and suitably elaborated and altered. Thus the Messiah is transformed into a person like the Son of man in Daniel. The Messiah is thus described and understood in terms drawn from the vision in Daniel 7. For this to happen suggests to me that there was a kind of Son of man concept without the actual phrase being used as a title. It was possible to take a specific set of ideas and apply them to the Messiah.

The same is true for the Similitudes in 1 Enoch. Here the Elect One, who is eventually identified with Enoch himself, is referred to as "that man," and the language of Daniel 7 is used to describe him. This seems to be much the same as in 4 Ezra. In other words we have two examples of the Messiah being described in terms taken from Daniel 7.

Second, while it may be enough for our purpose to show that this individualizing "messianic" use of the Son of man took place, the fact that it happened suggests that the Jewish tradition took Son of man in an individualizing, messianic sense, and it raises the question whether this interpretation of Daniel 7 may represent what was in fact the intention of the passage itself rather than being a secondary and mistaken interpretation. The case that the figure in Daniel 7 symbolizes the saints of the Most High in the sense that it symbolises their leader still seems to me to make the best sense of the passage.[36]

This early interpretation of the passage may well suggest how it would be interpreted in the time of Jesus. What we have is the use of the imagery of Daniel 7 to refer to a messianic type of figure, even though the actual phrase is not used as a title or designation. Consequently, when the phrase is used with a Danielic reference in the Gospels, then it carries with it this individual, messianic reference and implies a figure who is granted authority by God. The authority is supreme; sitting at the right hand of God is the highest status.

If we accept this view, then the following possibilities arise:

1. Jesus shared the kind of understanding of the figure current in some circles in the first century. He saw himself as having a future role at the judgment, identified himself with the manlike figure, and believed that he would have the authority of that figure.[37]

2. At the same time, we cannot ignore the other material which suggegts that Jesus had a remarkable consciousness of a filial relationship to God. These two types of self-understanding cannot be separated. Cumulatively, they imply that Jesus did have a consciousness of, and did claim at least in the presence of his disciples—a relationship and status without equal.

3. The question then arises as to how this is related to the concept of incarnation as developed by the church. By some point the church came to think of Jesus as a being appropriately called the Son of God or the Word who had come into the world after a previous phase of heavenly existence. The Son of man language in Daniel could be undertood in this way to refer to a heavenly figure in human form. It could have provided a vehicle for thinking along these lines. This point would be strengthened if the Danielic vision is to be understood as an apotheosis, the recognition or perhaps installation of a being with powers equal to those of God. Such a self-understanding on the part of Jesus is credible.

The question whether the concept of Son of man implies "pre-existence" has tended to be given a negative answer. The positive answer was defended by R. G. Hallerton-Kelly who explored a number of other concepts which might point in the same direction.

His case has not proved persuasive to other scholars.[38] However, the Elect One, alias "that man", who is identified with Enoch in 1 Enoch, is a pre-existent figure,[39] and the same would appear to be true of the man from the sea in 4 Ezra 13:26. The Son of man is certainly regarded as a pre-existent figure in John. In John 3 the Son of man has come down from heaven, and ascends to heaven. John appears to use Dan 7 to argue for a descent from God, and in the light of what has preceded in the Gospel the Son of man is here regarded as a divine figure. Previously in 1:51 the Son of man is a bridge-figure between heaven and earth. All this suggests that the concept of the Danielic Son of man conveyed the thought of a pre-existent being in the first century, although it has to be admitted that this thought is not developed or regarded as significant in the Synoptic Gospels.

It is thus arguable that the Son of man concept could be and was fitted harmoniously into a Christology involving the pre-existence of the Son of God. This step was taken in the NT. Whether it was taken by Jesus remains uncertain. It is, however, consistent with his self-understanding as the Son of God.

V. CONCLUSION

This paper has covered a lot of ground in a tentative fashion. We have examined the case that Jesus used the Aramaic phrase *barĕnash(a)* purely as a self-designation, in which case the term itself says virtually nothing about his self-understanding, but the things which Jesus says about himself in the rest of the sayings remain significant for his self-understanding. However, we argued that other teaching of Jesus suggests that this case needs re-examination and that it is likely that Jesus did claim authority of a high order from God. We then considered the Son of man sayings which refer to the future role of Jesus and saw that these could be credibly interpreted as indicating a messianic role which Jesus believed that he was to fulfill. If so, this has important consequences for his self-understanding during his earthly life. Whether the term carried implications of pre-existence in the actual teaching of Jesus remains uncertain.

It will be apparent that on the view which is criticized here the use of Son of man reflects a self-understanding of Jesus as a purely human figure with a prophetic calling from God. On the view which is put forward for discussion as doing better justice to the evidence, Jesus is seen as a figure conscious of a unique calling to be the Messianic agent of God. The term "Son of man" thus functions in an extraordinarily impressive way as one which binds together the relationships of Jesus to God and to the human race, and it sums up, as no other Christological expression does, the concept of Jesus as God incarnate in human form.

This paper has unfortunately done less than was promised in analyzing these alternatives and implications; hopefully it may lead into constructive discussion of them.

NOTES

1. B. Lindars, *Jesus Son of Man* (London: SPCK, 1983) 170.

2. D. R. A. Hare, *The Son of Man Tradition* (Minneapolis: Fortress, 1990) 200. With this position we may contrast that of R. G. Hamerton-Kelly, who in his study of *Pre-existence. Wisdom and the*

Son of Man (Cambridge University Press, 1973) 101, argued that "when Jesus used the self-designation 'Son of Man,' he and his hearers understood it to imply his pre-existence".

3. Since our aim in this paper is to assess the significance of the Son of man question for Christology, no attempt has been made to cover the discussion exhaustively, and I have not taken account of several important contributions. The literature on the subject is becoming almost inexhaustible, and I dare not pretend even to have consulted it all.

4. I have not yet been able to see the full discussion of D. Burkett, *The Son of Man in the Gospel of John* (Sheffield Academic Press, 1991). We can basically ignore the rest of the NT where the phrase is not found.

5. This simple analysis into three stages is complicated by the following factors:

a. Jesus may have said the same or similar things more than once with slightly different nuances. This important point is often ignored.

b. The oral transmission passed through several stages, and a saying may have been modified in wording and meaning not just once but several times.

c. The written history of a saying may also be multiple, in that the Evangelists may have used written sources.

d. Some stages in the process may be absent. A saying may have been created at stage b. or stage c. rather than going back to Jesus.

6. See D. R. A. Hare, op. cit. Essentially the same approach is adopted by J. D. Kingsbury, *Conflict in Luke: Jesus, Authorities, Disciples* (Minneapolis: Fortress, 1991) 73-8.

7. I have discussed the validity of these and other theories in earlier essays "The Synoptic Son of Man Sayings in Recent Discussion," *NTS* 12 (1965-66) 327-351; "The Son of Man in Contemporary Debate." *EQ* 42 (1970) 67-87. See further my summary treatment in J. B. Green (et al.), *Dictionary of Jesus and the Gospels* (Downers Grove: IVP, 1992) s.v. "Son of Man").

8. The NRSV in its attempt to avoid sexist language uses this phrase, but where the figure intended is undoubtedly male I reckon this is a misleading rendering.

9. *Jesus the Jew* (London: Collins, 1973).

10. *Son of Man: The Interpretation and Influence of Daniel 7* (London: SPCK, 1979); *From Jewish Prophet to Gentile God* (Cambridge: James Clarke, 1991).

11. *Jesus Son of Man* (London: SPCK, 1983).

12. Lindars' list varies slightly. He omits Mk 2:28; 8:38; 9:12; adds 9:31 (core only) and Lk 11:30 (diff. Mt 12:40); omits Lk 22:48.

13. Hare, who shares Vermes' understanding of the Aramaic idiom, lists as authentic: Mt 11:19 = Lk 7:34); Lk 12:10 (= Mt 12:32); Lk, 12:8f. (cf. Mt 10:32f.); Mt 8:20 (= Lk 9:58); Lk 11:30 (cf. Mt 12:40); Mk 2:10; the passion sayings. This is essentially the same as Lindars' list.

14. M. Casey, *From Jewish Prophet to Gentile God*. 48.

15. M. Casey, op. cit., 55.

16. B. Lindars, op. cit., 171.

17. B. Lindars, op. cit., 187.

18. The view of Vermes that Jesus is making statements that were true only of himself is obviously not vulnerable to this objection.

19. Jesus speaks about his forthcoming death using both 'I"-statements and *barenash(a)* statements.

20. It seems to me that several of the sayings are simply not valid as general statements (nos. 1., 4., 6., 7. [by virtue of its link with 6.], 8., and 9.). At the most, no more than five of the sayings have any degree of plausibility as general sayings, and they make equally good, indeed better sense when true of Jesus primarily or alone.

21. For further discussion of this point see my forthcoming essay "An Assessment of Some Recent Study of the Son of Man in the Synoptic Gospels."

22. Nevertheless, there remain some problems about the nature of the idiom. Was it used solely in the kind of situations suggested by Vermes? Is the evidence for its existence and use in the first century sufficiently strong? The whole question of whether an Aramaic idiom is being used

needs more discussion. Its existence in the Gospels is sharply questioned by C. C. Caragounis, *The Son of Man* (Tübingen: Mohr, 1986). See further B. Witherington, III, *The Christology of Jesus* (Minneapolis: Fortress, 1990) 236-8.

23. Thus we can regard as editorial: Mt 16:13 , 28; 24:30a; 26:2 (16:13 and 26:2 may be simple self-designations). There are a further 5 places in special Matthaean material where its originality is uncertain (Mt 10:23; 13:37, 41; 19:28 (diff. Lk 22:30); 25:31). In the Q material the use of Son of man in Lk 6:22 (diff. Mt 5:11) and Lk 12:8 (diff. Mt 10:32-3) is more likely to be original. Lk 24:7 is a report by the angels at the tomb of what Jesus said, and therefore is not really a separate saying.

24. M. Casey has affirmed this repeatedly, claiming that the emphatic state of the phrase remained generic. However, C. Colpe (TDNT VIII, 404 n. 24) claims that the Gospel usage supports the view that the determinate form "became normative for "the man' in the messianic sense."

25. Note that Jesus does not use the first person to speak of his future role, except in Mt 10:32f. where it may well be that Matthew has replaced an original Son of man reference.

26. J. D. G. Dunn, *Christology in the Making* (Philadelphia: Westminster Press 1981) 86f.

27. Our argument is that the case that Jesus could not have referred to himself in terms of the Son of man in Dan 7 is not compelling. The question that needs fuller discussion is whether there are positive grounds for believing that he did so quite apart from the fact that the Evangelists claim that he did so.

28. For this view see (among others) M. D. Hooker, *The Son of Man in Mark* (London: SPCK, 1967).

29. Cf. the discussion of Mk 2:28 above.

30. op. cit., 71f.

31. TDNT VIII, 400-477.

32. M. Black, "Die Apotheose Israels: eine neue Interpretation des danielischen 'Menschensohns'." in R. Pesch et al., *Jesus und der Menschensohn. Für Anton Vögtle* (Freiburg: Herder, 1975) 92-9.

33. F. F. Bruce, *The Real Jesus* (London: Hodder, 1985) 58-66.

34. op. cit., 74.

35. M. Casey, op. cit., 129.

36. G. R. Beasley-Murray, "The Interpretation of Daniel 7" CBQ 45, (1983), 44-58; *Jesus and the Kingdom of God* (Exeter: Paternoster, 1986) 26-35. D. R. A. Hare, op. cit., 10-21, allows that 4 Ezra has a messianizing interpretation, but claims that it does not evidence a supernatural Son of man. Similarly with 1 Enoch. But this allows the basic point that we are making, namely, that there was a messianic interpretation in the first century .

37. The view that Jesus was influenced by Dan 7 and that he understood himself in terms of the figure described there, is not without its supporters, and has been upheld by C. Caragounis and S. Kim.

38. J. D. G. Dunn, op. cit.

39. M. Casey, "The Use of the Term 'Son of Man' in the Similitudes of Enoch." JSJ 7 (1976) 11-29.

ONE GOD, ONE LORD, ONE PEOPLE

Incarnational Christology for a Church in a Pagan Environment

N. T. WRIGHT

I. INTRODUCTION

My aim in this paper is to examine a theme and context which is often marginalized but which, arguably, stands as close as any other to the heart of Paul's theology. I refer to the question of meat offered to idols, discussed in 1 Corinthians 8-10. My argument is, I hope, fairly simple. It is that Paul, in this passage, offers the Corinthian church, surrounded as it was by paganism, a Christological center for its belief and action, which relates directly and in a challenging manner to the task of confronting paganism with the gospel. Though the question of meat offered to idols has often been thought to have little contemporary relevance, I hope to show that the passage is not only exegetically fascinating and theologically thought provoking, but possesses more potential relevance to the church and the world of the late twentieth century than might at first sight be imagined.

In mounting this argument I shall draw on two other studies. The initial focal point of the passage is 1 Corinthians 8: 6, which is one of Paul's most remarkable Christological formulations. I have expounded the technicalities of the verse elsewhere, and here presuppose some of that detailed argumentation.[1] Similarly, I have argued in a forthcoming work that the task of the contemporary church involves a serious addressing of the multi-faceted paganism that is rapidly replacing post-enlightenment Deism or atheism as the major feature of modern Western culture, and I likewise presuppose some of that discussion.[2]

II. THE CORINTHIAN SITUATION

Studies of Corinth have abounded recently, and for our purposes amount to the obvious and major conclusion: Corinth was a thoroughly pagan city, typical of many in the ancient world.[3] This did not, of course, mean merely that most of the inhabitants went from time to time to worship at pagan shrines and temples. It meant that the world view of the entire town was dominated by pagan assumptions, that the visual appearance of the town was dominated by pagan symbolism, that the normal mind set of the average Corinthian was dominated by pagan ideas, pagan hopes, and pagan motivations, and that the normal life style was dominated by pagan practices. Although the modern Western world is, I believe, moving towards a rediscovery of paganism at quite an alarming rate, it still requires something of a mental effort to reconstruct the picture of a city such as Corinth.[4]

There was, of course, a sizeable Jewish population in the town, as was true pretty well all around the Mediterranean. How influential this community was we have no means of knowing. Nor is it clear to what extent the Jewish community in Corinth would have clung to some kind of Pharisaic orthodoxy in their belief and behavior, or to what extent they would have been open to new, perhaps Hellenistic, ideas. It is clear, though, that their twin beliefs, monotheism and election, cut clean across all the normal assumptions of paganism. It is in this clash between Judaism and paganism that we find the true background to Paul's argument in 1 Corinthians, not least in chapters 8-10.

Jewish monotheism in this period was not a speculative doctrine about the inner being of the one true god.[5] It was the polemical belief that there was only one god, the creator of the whole world, and that all other gods were simply idols, human inventions with possible demonic associations. This belief is to be clearly distinguished from other ancient varieties of monotheism, notably Stoic pantheism. There is all the difference in the world between saying that there is one god because everything that exists is god, and saying that there is one god who *made* everything that exists. And this Jewish creational monotheism was linked closely with the belief that this one creator god had called Israel to be his special people. Israel's central theology thus equipped her to face the ravages of pagan oppression in the period between the Babylonian exile and the first century, and indeed the events of this period served to strengthen her grip on the belief in her god as the one true god, who would eventually vindicate his name and his people against all other gods and their adherents.

The choices facing Jews in the pagan world were therefore quite stark. One option was to withdraw from contact with the world, to retreat into the ghetto. The problem with this was the strong Jewish belief in the goodness of creation: treating large areas of the world as off limits went against the grain (for instance) of the Psalms with their celebration of the created order. Retreat into dualism, though it often happened, could never represent a wholeheartedly Jewish solution. The other option was of course to assimilate. Jews from that day to this have faced this possibility, and we may presume that then as now some would lose their identity completely, while others would find various compromise solutions. But at the heart of the whole issue we will always find the theological and ethical questions which serve as shorthand for these large socio-cultural issues. Questions of monotheism versus polytheism, questions of the identity of the people of the one God, and questions of behavior with respect to food, drink and sex: these are not merely matters of an abstract theology or ethics, but relate to the entire world view, the entire way of being-in-the-world, of people in the ancient, and I believe the modern world.

III. THE HEART OF PAUL'S RESPONSE: CHRISTOLOGY

With this, we turn to the substantive issue that faced Paul. Should Christians in Corinth eat meat that had been offered to idols? We should be clear how far-reaching the question actually was. Though there is some debate about details, it seems likely that almost all the meat available in a city like Corinth would have been offered at some shrine or other; and idol-temples served not only as butcher's shops but also as restaurants.[6] To avoid idol meat altogether might, then, mean *de facto* vegetarianism (an option forced on some in any case by economic circumstances). For a Jew, facing this question would pose quite sharply the options we just noted. One major Jewish position regarded pagan worship as idolatry, and insisted that genuine monotheists must not flirt with it. Another major Jewish tradition said that idols were non existent and irrelevant, and that the one creator god claimed as his own all that idols have usurped. This second way may well have been helped by the kind of speculative Jewish *gnosis* according to which one's relationship to the one true god elevated one above the problems of the pagan world.[7] The first way could lead to dualism, the second to assimilation. Paul carves out a way which avoids both.

He refuses to discuss the question in terms merely of a practical agenda. He goes (much more readily than some of his commentators) to the substantive issue that lies behind it all, that is, monotheism and idolatry. He does not work with the categories of a post-Reformation agenda, asking whether the "law"is a good thing or a bad thing, debating earnestly about whether "ethics" and "morality" somehow compromise the gospel of free grace. And, despite some recent writers who have suggested that he is simply shooting from the hip, offering haphazard and inconsistent solutions to problems as they come up, I suggest that his solution is actually clear, theologically grounded, and strikingly relevant.[8] He offers the church a redefinition of monotheism and election, both achieved by means of his central Christology; and he shows how this redefinition of fundamental Jewish theology enables the church not merely to survive and maintain its identity vis-a-vis paganism but to take on paganism and, in a sense, beat it at its own game. He offers, in short, an incarnational theology for a church in a pagan environment.

This helps to explain the beginning of the argument (8:1-3). Paul responds to the claim to *gnosis* by insisting on the primacy of Jewish style allegiance to the one true god, as expressed in the central Jewish prayer, the *Shema* ("'Hear, O Israel, the Lord our God, the Lord is One, and thou shalt love the Lord thy God. . .");

> Concerning idol meat, we know that "we all have *gnosis.*" Gnosis puffs you up, but love builds you up. Anyone who claims to "know" something does not yet have the necessary "knowledge"; but anyone who "loves God" is known by God (vv. 1-3)

Paul is about to quote the *Shema* explicitly, in v. 4, but he clearly has it in mind already. The question at stake in the discussion of idol meat is, who are the people of God? The Jewish answer is: who says the *Shema*? Paul begins by affirming this answer, before introducing a striking new dimension:

> Concerning meat offered to idols, then, we know that "there is no idol in the world," and that "there is no god but one" (v. 4).

Monotheism is what matters. But this credal statement by itself hardly addresses the situation on the street in Corinth, so he continues:

> Well, though, there may be many so-called gods, whether in heaven or on earth— just as there are many "gods" and many "lords"— . . . (v. 5).

The pagan pantheon is not irrelevant. It must be confronted. One cannot retreat from paganism, just as one must not assimilate. One must instead worship the true God, the one whom paganism parodies. This, I shall suggest, is in fact the heart of the whole argument. And for Paul this true God is revealed in Jesus of Nazareth.

In what is surely one of the most striking Christological formulations ever written in any century, Paul takes an argument which is about monotheism, and takes the Jewish formula which is the most basic expression of Jewish monotheism, and places Jesus at the heart of it. Instead of

> Hear, O Israel: the Lord our God, the Lord is One

we have

> But for us:
> One God
> the father, from whom are all things and we to him
> and one Lord
> Jesus the Messiah,
> through whom are all things and through whom are we. (8:6)

This is all the more striking when we put the Septuagint of Deuteronomy 6:4 beside the Greek of Paul's formula:

> *akoue Israel, kyrios ho theos hēmōn eis estiv*

What Paul seems to have done is as follows. He has expanded the formula, in a way quite unprecedented in any other texts known to us, so as to include a gloss on *théos* and another on *Kurios*:[9]

> *all hēmin*
> *eis theos ho patēr*
> *ex ou ta pavta kai eis autov*
> *kai eis kurios Iesous Christos*
> *di ou ta pavta kai hēmeis di autou*

Paul, in other words, has glossed "God" with "the Father," and "Lord" with "Jesus Christ," adding in each case an explanatory phrase: "God" is the Father, "from whom are all things and we to him," and the "Lord" is Jesus the Messiah, "through whom are all things and we through him." There can be no mistake: Paul has placed Jesus *within* an explicit statement, drawn from the Old Testament's best known monotheistic text, of the doctrine that Israel's God is the one and only God, the creator of the world. The *Shema* was already, at this stage of Judaism, in widespread use as the Jewish daily prayer.[10] Paul has redefined it Christologically, producing what we can only call a sort of Christological monotheism.

IV. CHRISTOLOGY, THEREFORE LOVE

It would be easy, though mistaken, to get so excited about Paul's astonishing Christological innovation that one would miss the point of this Christology within the over-all argument. We have already seen that he is reasserting Jewish style monotheism over against the pagan polytheism of Corinth. But what practical difference does this redefinition make, when it comes to the question of idol meat?

The question, as we saw, was first and foremost an issue of the definition of the community of the people of god. Living as we do in a period of atomized individualism, it is necessary for us to think our way back into the first century, where individual behavior was seen for what more recent sociologists of knowledge have been insisting it really is: one function of communal life.[11] Paul addresses the issue at this level, applying his reformulated monotheism to the question. What does it mean to be the true people of *this* one god?

It means, clearly, that love and concern for other members of the community is to be placed ahead of all attempts at personal self-realization. In 8:7-13 he spells this out in terms precisely of the Christ who has become part of the definition of the one god, the Christ who is identical with the Jesus who died on the cross:

> Since some have become so accustomed to idols until now, they still think of the food they eat as food offered to an idol; and their conscience, being weak, is defiled. "Food will not bring us close to God." We are no worse off if we do not eat, and no better off if we do. But take care that this liberty of yours does not somehow become a stumbling block to the weak. For if others see you, who possess knowledge, eating in the temple of an idol, might they not, since their conscience is weak, be encouraged to the point of eating food sacrificed to idols? So by your knowledge those weak believers for whom Christ died are destroyed. But when you thus sin against members of your family, and wound their conscience when it is weak, you sin against Christ. Therefore, if food is a cause of their falling, I will never eat meat, so that I may not cause one of them to fall (vv. 7-13).

The *gnosis* of which some members of the community are proud, namely, their knowledge of the one true God, must, if it really *is* the true God they are worshipping, bring them immediately to the realization that this true God, in the person of the Messiah, died to rescue both them and the rest from precisely those evils of which paganism is clearly symptomatic. Though the word *agape* itself does not occur in this passage, that is what it is all about: the love of the true God for his people, and the consequent love that this people must show, not only for him in private religion, but also for him in the persons of the rest of the family. The corporate sense of *Christos* is clearly visible under v.12: sinning against a member of the family is sinning against the Messiah, in whom this family is summed up.[12] And the whole effect is to put into practice the *Shema* itself: there is one God, one Lord, and his people are defined as those who love him, and who love their neighbors as themselves. The allowance for the weak is not a mere *ad hoc* concession. It arises from the heart of Christian theology itself. Hence 1 Corinthians 13 can be seen as a climax of the whole letter, a full dress exposition of what is needed when facing the pagan world.

V. CHRISTOLOGY, THEREFORE ABANDONMENT OF RIGHTS

It is at this point that 1 Corinthians 9 makes its proper impact. The sudden change of topic, from a discussion of idol meat to a discussion of Paul's apostleship and its outworking, has inevitably led some scholars to question the integrity of the passage.

This has been further compounded by the fact that the advice in chapter 10 on the subject of idol meat does not seem the same as that in chapter 8. But if we follow the line we have begun, we will discover that beneath these apparent discrepancies there is a coherence born of the theology which Paul is in fact expounding, and which usually goes unnoticed.

The reason why Paul suddenly launches into a discussion of his apostleship may have something to do with a defence against those who are marginalizing him and looking to some other leader(s) instead (cf. 1 Corinthians 1:10-17; 3:1-23). But if this is so it is strictly a subplot to the main theme of the passage. Paul's basic intention is to offer himself as the example of how to approach such issues, where one has a right to do something but deliberately makes no use of that right for the sake of the gospel. He sums this up in 11.1: "Be imitators of me, as I am of Christ." Here again the redefined monotheism of 1 Corinthians 8:6 works its way out into actual practice.

If it were not for 11:1, this conclusion might be resisted. Nowhere in 1 Corinthians 9 does Paul say explicitly that in abandoning his rights he is following the example of the Messiah.[13] But here a parallel passage comes to our aid. In Philippians 2:1-11, we find first (vv. 1-4) a clear exhortation to do exactly what Paul says in our present passage that he is doing himself, namely, to give up one's rights for one another's sake; and that passage is at once buttressed by Philippians 2:5-11, in which Paul describes Jesus the Messiah as the one who did precisely that. Moreover, Philippians 2:5-11 is one of the other two passages in Paul (the third one is Colossians 1:15-20) in which Paul takes explicit Jewish monotheistic texts and themes and puts Jesus at the middle of them.[14] The incarnational Christology of Philippians 2: 5-11 thus undergirds explicitly the appeal that Christians should give up their own rights for one anothers' sake. What we have in 1 Corinthians 8 and 9, I suggest, is the same theme spelt out in one particular way. To the question, should we exercise our God-given liberty and, scorning idols as nonexistent irrelevancies, go ahead and eat meat that has been offered to them? Paul makes three replies:

> 1) First get your monotheism straight; it is true that there is only one God, but this God is now made known in and through Jesus the Messiah, and in loving this God you may find that there are other more pressing duties than showing your contempt for idols by eating their food without caring.
>
> 2) Then recognize that among these more urgent need needs is to care for those who are struggling in the faith, and that this may mean happily forgoing your demonstration of monotheism in terms of eating idol meat in favor of a demonstration of this redefined monotheism in terms of abstaining from idol meat.
>
> 3) then recognize that in this abstention, too, you are demonstrating that you are the people of this one true God, since in Jesus this God gave up his rights to come and rescue you too.

The cross, therefore, stands clearly underneath this argument. For Paul, the crucifixion of Jesus does not simply have to do with the attaining of individual salvation. It means the remaking of the community of the people of god in a particular fashion, namely, as the community that is given such security in the love of the true god that it is able to forgo all human privileges and rights to which it might otherwise lay claim. What is more, Paul saw clearly that the cross, in achieving this, offers the most fundamental challenge to paganism at every level. This is, I believe, the real subtext of our present passage. Instead of asking "'how far can we go?" in apparent assimilation to paganism, Paul shows a different agenda altogether. The monotheism which has been redefined so as to have Jesus, and hence the cross, at its heart, is the monotheism which not only provides a way for its adherents to live within a pagan world with integrity, but which also issues to that pagan world a decisive and devastating challenge (compare 1 Corinthians 2:6-8). Instead of merely pursuing a path of private spirituality *within* the world, the church is to pursue a path of mission *to* the world. And the victory which is to be won by that mission is the victory of the cross.

Paganism, at its heart, powerfully reinforced the boundaries of nation, family and tribe, of geography and gender, that crisscrossed the ancient world. It is a striking fact that, apart from within Judaism, we have little or no evidence in the ancient world of what we today call "charity"; there was no sense of obligation to the poor, except to the poor among one's own kin or among those who might be of political usefulness. Though the word "charity" has of course become cold and hard, we might pause to imagine a world from which the very notion had been removed. It would be colder and harder yet. And that is the world that Paul was challenging with the gospel of Jesus. The church is summoned, as the very stuff of its life, not as an added extra when private spirituality has been sorted out, to incarnate that love, that charity, just as the God it professes to worship had done. And in that process the church must watch out for the signs that underneath a professed adherence to monotheism there is not a self-centeredness that must itself be challenged by the cross: "I punish my body and enslave it," writes Paul, "so that after proclaiming to others I myself should not be disqualified" 1 Corinthians 9:27. A spirituality that does not contain at least the possibility of such an attitude stands under the warning that, though professing Christianity, it may in fact have embraced some form of paganism.[15] Insisting on one's rights, even insisting on one's rights as a Christian, is a sign that something else other than the true God is being worshipped. The Christology of 1 Corinthians 8:6 thus undergirds the exposition of paradoxical apostleship in 1 Corinthians 9, and prepares the way for the return to the main topic in 1 Corinthians 10.

VI. CHRISTOLOGY AND THE TRUE FEEDING

Rather than simply sketch out a position which helps Christians to get round the problem of idol meat, Paul now goes boldly on to the attack. He puts at the center of the picture the true Christian eating and drinking, of which pagan feasting is a mere parody. This is, in fact, his regular critique of paganism. Avoiding pagan life styles by avoiding the raw material in which they deal is dualism; assimilating to those life styles is to abandon allegiance to the one God. The genuine alternative to both ways is to embrace the gospel as the reality of which paganism is the distorted copy. And this means seeing pagan feasting in the light of the eucharist.

I am not aware that 1 Corinthians 10 is normally read in this light, but I suggest that it ought to be. The whole chapter is about religious meals, how they function, and what they imply. Paul begins with the Jewish meals, the"spiritual" feeding in the wilderness (vv.1-13), and moves on to the Christian eucharist (vv. 14-17), in order then to draw out his final, nuanced, response to the problem at hand (vv. 18 - 11:1). In doing this he is,

I suggest, following a pattern of argument similar to that which we observed in the foundational passage, 1 Corinthians 8:1-6.

First, he claims the Jewish ground. Just as in chapter 8 he began with the *Shema,* so in chapter 10 he begins with Passover. Monotheism in chapter 8 is thus balanced by the wilderness feedings in chapter 10 ("our ancestors. . . all ate the same spiritual food, and all drank the same spiritual drink" (vv.1- 3). Faced with paganism, Paul always begins his thought as a loyal Jew. In both cases, the overtones of Passover are not far away. The *Shema* recalls the god who brought Israel out of Egypt. The desert feedings result from the same great act of liberation. Passover and Exodus likewise come together in the Christian antitype, the eucharist.

Second, he shows that this approach by itself did not save the Jews from assimilation to pagan practices. In the earlier passage, this comes by implication: the Jewish-Hellenistic *gnosis* of which some are so proud will lead them, if they are not careful, into assimilation. In the present passage, in explicit detail, he shows that the earlier feeding of the Jews did not prevent idolatry (v.7), immorality (v.8), treating the Lord as a pagan deity (v.9),[16] and grumbling that their god had not behaved properly towards them (v.10). So, while claiming the Jewish heritage not only for himself but for his erstwhile pagan converts ("our ancestors," v.1), he sees that one must go further. Judaism by itself is not enough.

Third, he goes on to assert the Christian truth which is, in his view, the fulfillment of the Jewish truth, and which thus claims the high ground that paganism had been trying to occupy. In 1 Corinthians 8, this move consists in his redefinition of the Jewish *Shema* so that it becomes the answer to pagan polytheism. The religion of "gods many and lords many" is replaced by the one God, the one Lord. In 1 Corinthians 10:16-17, this Christology opens up to reveal, in a nutshell, the meaning of the Christian eucharist, containing as it does echoes of older Jewish liturgies,[17] and offering the decisive alternative to all pagan ritual meals:

> The cup of blessing which we bless
>   is it not a sharing in the blood of Christ?
> The bread which we break
>   is it not a sharing in the body of Christ?
> Because there is one bread, we who are many are one body
>   for we all partake of the one bread.[18]

The redefinition of monotheism by means of Jesus has given birth to a redefinition of the one people of the true god; and this one people is revealed precisely in their sharing of the meal by which they constitute themselves as such. If there is one God, and one Lord, then those who celebrate and worship this one God and Lord become one people, *transcending* differences of race, gender, class and geography. This celebration resembles pagan feasts simply in the way that the sun is like a lightbulb: the former is the reality of which the latter is a copy invented by humans.

To modern protestant or rationalist eyes, Paul's description of this celebration could look as though it was sailing close to the wind of assimilation, that is, assimilation to paganism. Just as critics of Paul's incarnational Christology have accused him of selling his Jewish birthright for a mess of pagan or gnostic polytheism,[19] so critics of his eucharistic theology are bound to accuse him of making the eucharist just like a form of paganism. But at this point protestantism, rationalism and Judaism, if they make this accusation, are standing on dangerously dualistic ground. From Paul's point of view it is paganism that apes the true sacramental worship, not the other way round. The function of this eucharistic passage within the present argument is to say: in the central Christian mystery you become one family through sharing in the blood and body of Christ, so how can you then share in the cup, or the table, of antigods, of nongods, or of demons? Verse 16 is explicitly applied in verse 21:

> You cannot drink the cup of the Lord and the cup of demons. You cannot partake of the table of the Lord and the table of demons.

The argument of chapter 10 as a whole, then, pivots on the eucharistic passages just as chapter 8 pivoted on the Christological reformulation. Those who take the redefined monotheism seriously are bound to follow it through by their love for one another. This Christology, and this love, find their ritual expression in the eucharist; and those who take this redefined community meal seriously are bound to follow it through into a life of holiness, in which attendance at idol temples is abjured.

A note at this point may be in order about Paul's exact view of idols. He has already agreed with the "strong" in Corinth that idols have no existence as such (8:4), and he is clear in the present passage that he is not retracting this earlier point (10:19). But this does not rule out the possibility that malign nonhuman entities not only may exist, but may gain power through pagan ritual and then exercise that power over humans, even over Christians. Paul (or one of his earliest interpreters) clearly believed that Christians take part in an ongoing battle to implement the victory of Jesus over the powers of darkness (Ephesians 6:10-20; Colossians 2:15). To worship in an idol's temple would therefore be to flirt with, or give the appearance of flirting with, the very powers that continue to enslave and distort human existence. These powers ought, instead, to be challenged by the gospel of liberation and healing. Such powers are not to be thought of as rivals to the one God, one Lord. That is the message both of 1 Corinthians 8:4-6 and Colossians 1:15-20. To forget this is to court dualism indeed. But this does not mean that Christians must not take the powers very seriously. Instead of asking, as the Corinthians' question implicitly asks, to what extent one is allowed to fraternize with them, one ought to be asking how their remaining power over humans can be broken.

Paul's answer to this question comes in the radical application of the cross to all human and Christian life. Victory over the powers comes, not from human wisdom, from success in human terms, but from the forswearing of all kinds of human power and authority, privilege and status. When Christians in Corinth and elsewhere give up their rights, they are not merely retreating from human possibility out of generous concern for one another. They are striking a blow against the paganism which offers humans a spurious self-worth, an inflated self-identity.[20] They are offering a direct challenge to paganism, based not on their own new-found religious self-assurance but on the revelation of the one god, one lord which they have discovered in the cross. They are doing what (I suggest) all Christian confrontation of paganism must do. Instead of either assimilating or retreating into a dualistic ghetto, the church must seek to build shrines for the true god on ground at present occupied by paganism. Only so can the dehumanizing and distorting power of paganism be broken, and replaced with the healing and restoring love of the creator and redeemer god.

Paul's answer to the Corinthians' problem can therefore be set out as follows:

1) What is at stake in the issue of idol meat is the question of monotheism and election, over against paganism.

2) Embracing Jewish-style monotheism is the true challenge to paganism, and this monotheism finds its fulfillment in Jesus.

3) Creational monotheism means that all meat is in principle edible by Christians.

4) The Christological redefinition of monotheism means, however, that for the sake of those with weak consciences one may be under obligation to forgo this right.

5) The redefined monotheism is expressed in the redefined celebratory meal, which is the true alternative to pagan celebrations.

6) This meal must issue in holiness and wholeness.

7) Therefore, though eating meat bought in the market is in principle all right, eating in an idol's temple is not.

Paul has addressed a complex situation with a clear theology. Paganism is to be challenged with a redefined doctrine, and practice, of monotheism and election.

VII. CONCLUSION: CHRISTOLOGY IN PRACTICE

It should have become clear by now that the reconstruction of Pauline Christology, and the detailed exegesis by which that task is to be accomplished, is very far from being a matter merely of antiquarian interest. Nor is it simply a matter of dotting the i's and crossing the t's of some abstract dogmatic scheme. It has to do with the very practical matter of living out the gospel within a pagan society. And that, I suggest, is increasingly the concern of the church in the modern Western world. Those of us who cut our exegetical teeth on Galatians and Romans, dealing as they do with questions at issue between Christianity and Judaism, may now find ourselves invited to get to grips with those parts of the Pauline correspondence where the battle with paganism is more specifically joined. We must hammer out the whole Pauline world view, not just a few abstract theological issues, in terms of Paul's central redefinitions of Jewish monotheism and election by means of Christ and the Spirit. And we must remember as we do so that the point of monotheism and election in the first place was that it was the creator's answer to paganism. All of this results, I think, in four closely related agendas.

First, the church must recapture the sense of celebration within the eucharist. At the risk of being thought (by dualists) to be sailing close to the wind of paganism, we must celebrate in bread and wine the true God of whom any corn-king or Bacchus is simply a parody. We must participate in the Messiah by feeding at his table and drinking his cup, aware that in doing so we are drawing upon his own risen life to sustain us in our own struggle against the powers of paganism. (Is it significant that the countries in which rationalistic protestantism has made most advance have been those where overt paganism has given way, until recently, to Deism?) In the eucharist we not only remember a past event. We worship, and participate in the life of, the living god and lord revealed in the gospel.

Second, we must work out this celebration in terms of a practical *holiness*. Holiness has all too often been thought of in dualistic terms, as abstention from things which are so tainted with misuse as to be thought evil in and of themselves. In reaction to this, the cult of modern Western self-fulfillment has pursued a path of personal *wholeness*, in which self-denial plays little or no part. What we need to do, and can do with the Christology and sacramental theology of 1 Corinthians behind us, is to embrace, articulate and exemplify a life path which embodies both. No idolatry; no immorality; and no dualism, either (10:7, 8, 23-7). "The earth is the Lord's, and the fullness thereof."

Third, we must comprehend, and work out in terms of Christian life and church structures, the bracing agenda of 1 Corinthians 9. What might it mean for Christians zealously to seek not to stand on their rights? The question is so enormous, and in our culture so novel, that it is difficult to answer. But one result would certainly follow. Such action would constitute a powerful challenge to the paganism which is gaining ground in our culture, as it prevailed at Corinth. It would be far more effective than "marches for Jesus" or fulminating sermons, both of which can easily become a cloak for insecurity and pride, which feed on one another within a church that has not fully grasped its own central Christology.

Finally, we must recapture the sense of excitement that ought properly to accompany serious Christological work. Those of us who grew up learning how to distinguish *homoousios* from *homoiousios* in Patristic debate may have come to feel that such tasks, however important both in their time and as an abstract exercise in thinking clearly and Christianly, are not strictly relevant to contemporary attempts to bring the gospel to the world. But we cannot retreat from the challenge that faces us in our own day, a challenge to grasp and articulate a Christologically redefined monotheism over against the paganism, the polytheism, and also the resurgent dualism within our own culture and church life. Paul discovered that the gospel of the crucified and risen Jesus contained "the power of God, and the wisdom of God" (1 Corinthians 1:24). We in our generation would do well to rediscover it too.

NOTES

1. See Wright 1991, ch. 6. I am also presupposing the work of commentators such as Conzelmann 1975 [1969], Fee 1987, Barrett 1971[1968] and Bruce 1971, and studies such as Willis 1985. [Editor's note: See bibliography at the end of the article for titles of these works.]

2. Wright 1992.

3. See Theissen 1982; Meeks 1983; Murphy-O'Connor 1983; and e.g. the introduction to Fee's commentary 1987, 1-4.

4. On paganism see particularly Lane Fox 1986.

5. In discussing the beliefs of pagans, Jews and Christians in the first century, it seems to me highly misleading to use the modern idiom of capitalizing the word "god," as though the word were univocal.

6. See Erhardt 1964, 279; Lane Fox 1986, 70. But cf. too Tomson 1990,189.

7. So Horsley 1978,1980; see my discussion and critique in Wright 1991, ch. 6.

8. E.g. Sanders 1983,1991.

9. See Wright 1986, 208; Hurtado 1988, 97 f.

10. Cf. mBer. 1 ff., etc.

11. See e.g. Berger and Luckman 1966; Berger 1969; Wilson 1982; and the discussion in Thiselton 1992, ch. 16 section 2.

12. See Wright 1991, chs. 2 and 3. Compare 1 Cor. 1:13; 12:12.

13. Verse 21 is a possible exception, where he speaks of being "under the law of Christ," but this by itself is too cryptic to be used as clear evidence.

14. See Wright 1991, chs. 4 and 5.

15. I think not least of the work of Matthew Fox, e.g. 1983.

16. Ignoring for the moment the nest of problems, textual and otherwise, in this verse.

17. On the "cup of blessing" as a Jewish formulation see Strack-Billerbeck 3. 419, 4. 627-36; see too Fee 467 f

18. I reserve judgment on whether this passage is or contains a pre-Pauline eucharistic formulation. What matters here is its function within the total argument of the chapter.

19. See particularly Maccoby 1986, 1991.

20. The phrase "puffed up," from the root *phusioo* is a feature of 1 Corinthians: cf 4:6,18,19; 5;2; 8:1; 13:4.

21. These conclusions are reinforced by the sequence of thought in chs. 5-7. There, as here, Paul sets his face against pagan practices, and also against the kind of asceticism that rejects the proper use of creation, and reaffirms the Jewish view (in this case, the goodness of marriage) within a Christian framework.

BIBLIOGRAPHY

Barrett, C. K. *A Commentary on the First Epistle to the Corinthians*. 2nd ed. Black's New Testament Commentaries. London: A. & C. Black, 1971 [1968].

Berger, Peter L. *The Sacred Canopy* New York: Doubleday, 1969.

Berger, Peter L., and Thomas Luckman. *The Social Construction of Reality: A Treatise in the Sociology of Knowledge*. Garden City: Doubleday, 1966.

Bruce, F. F. *1 and 2 Corinthians*. New Century Bible, London: Oliphants, 1971.

Conzelmann, Hans. *1 Corinthians: A Commentary on the First Epistle to the Corinthians*. Trans. James W. Leitch. Hermeneia. Philadelphia: Fortress Press, 1975 [1969].

Erhardt, A. *The Framework of the New Testament Stories*. Manchester: Manchester University Press, 1964.

Fee, Gordon D. *The First Epistle to the Corinthians*. Ed. F. F. Bruce. The New International Commentary on the New Testament. Grand Rapids: Eerdmans, 1987.

Fox, Matthew. *Original Blessing: A Primer in Creation Spirituality*. Santa Fe: Bear & Co., 1983.

Fox, Robin Lane. *Pagans and Christians*. New York/London: Alfred A. Knopf/Penguin, 1986.

Horsley, Richard A. "Consciousness and Freedom Among the Corinthians. "*Catholic Biblical Quarterly* 40 (1978): 574-589.

_____. "Gnosis in Corinth: I Corinthians 8.1-6" *New Testament Studies* 27 (1980): 32-51.

Hurtado, Larry W. *One God, One Lord: Early Christian Devotion and Ancient Jewish Monotheism*. Philadelphia: Fortress, 1988.

Maccoby, Hyam.*The Mythmaker: Paul and the Invention of Christianity*. London: Wiedenfeld and Nicolson, 1986.

_____*Paul and Hellenism*. London/Philadelphia: S.C.M. Press/Trinity Press International, 1991.

Meeks, Wayne A. *The First Urban Christians: The Social World of the Apostle Paul*. New Haven: Yale University Press, 1983.

Murphy-O'Connor, J. *St. Paul's Corinth: Texts and Archaeology*. Wilmington, DE: Michael Glazier, 1983.

Sanders, E. P. *Paul, the Law, and the Jewish People*. Philadelphia/London: Fortress/SCM Press, 1983.

_____. *Paul. Past Masters*.. Oxford: Oxford University Press, 1991.

Theissen, Gerd. *The Social Setting of Pauline Christianity: Essays on Corinth.* Ed. and trans. John H. Schutz. Philadelphia: Fortress, 1982.

Thiselton, Anthony C. *New Horizons in Hermeneutics: The Theory and Practice of Transforming Biblical Reading.* London/New York: Harper Collins, 1992.

Tomson, Peter J. *Paul and the Jewish Law: Halakha in the Letters of the Apostle to the Gentiles.* Compendia Rerum Iudaicarum ad Novum Testamentum, section III: Jewish traditions in early Christian literature, vol. 1. Assen/Minneapolis: Van Gorcum/Fortress Press, 1990.

Willis, Wendell Lee. *Idol Meat in Corinth: The Pauline Argument in I Corinthians 8 and 10* . Socciety of Biblical Literature Dissertation Series. Chico, California: Scholars Press, 1985.

Wilson, Bryan. *Religion in Sociological Perspective.* London: Oxford University Press, 1982.

Wright, N. T. "'Constraints' and the Jesus of History." *Scottish Journal of Theology* 39. (1986): 189-210.

———*The Climax of the Covenant: Christ and the Law in Pauline Theology.* Edinburgh: T & T Clark, 1991.

_____. *New Tasks for a Renewed Church.* London: Hodder and Stoughton, 1992.

Wonder, Worship and Writ: Patristic Christology

FREDERICK W. NORRIS

Perhaps like yours, my undergraduate and seminary years taught me summaries of classical Trinitarian and Christological formulae that emphasized the philosophical backgrounds of the major terms. Both standard church history and history of doctrine textbooks provided that perspective and quoted excerpts from the original sources. Trinity and Christology within this framework entailed grasping the meaning of *homoousios, homoiousios, ousia* and *hypostasis* as well as *natura* and *persona.* As I memorized what those terms meant I became confident that I understood what Trinity and Christology meant.

When, however, I was preparing for one of my special doctoral examinations which covered the first four ecumenical councils, I found something rather puzzling. The bulk of the treatises from the major writers, even the polemical ones, did not work out of a philosophical laboratory in which the truths of the various philosophical schools were made the judge of Christian doctrine. The more I read the primary literature the more it seemed that the magisterial secondary works on the history of Christian thought had concentrated too often on the development of doctrine through the use of ever more sophisticated philosophical terms. That observation marked the beginning of my understanding.

Now some twenty years later I only hope I understand. More and more my life is filled with wonder that comes from worshipful study of writ. I deny neither the development which the histories trace, nor that they have done well in mapping that development. What I want to suggest is that mature patristic views of Trinity and Christology, the attempts to explain the incarnation, are actually hermeneutical models; their original intent in the writings of many early Christian theologians was to make sense of those leaders' deep, living and worshipful memory of scripture. When you know that much scripture by heart what do you do with it? In a significant and yet secondary way those models also were framed to answer specific cultural questions. As models they could be talked about on their own, but their adequacy always depended upon their ability to bring together what was said variously and widely in scripture, to understand it within the church and to make it clear to specific audiences.

If that be true we must approach the great creeds with their obviously philosophically sophisticated words in two ways. First, it is quite unlikely that the classical formulas, three persons in one nature and two natures in one person, can ever be fully discarded. Claiming holy writ within the context of Christian worship makes that impossible. As some have said, if the creeds and the early theologians weren't there we would have to invent them. At the very least the creeds will remain both handy statements of the problems faced in interpreting scripture and short descriptions of the ways in which early theologians faced those issues and tried to state the center of Christian faith within their churches and to their cultures. Second, because the classical formulas must be read in context, there may be ways in which their wording should be adapted to our own contemporary settings. When we do that we will be following the example of early Christian leaders, not leaving them behind. Even in the midst of scathing polemical debate about the nature of orthodoxy and heresy, early Christian theologians often kept pagan religion and society in view as an important part of their audience.

To make this case I have chosen to look at two Greek fathers: Athanasius and Gregory of Nazianzus. Athanasius is the rock from which much of our orthodox faith is hewn; he defended the incarnation against a rather interesting and persuasive foe, Arius of Alexandria. Gregory of Nazianzus combatted the teachings of Aetius and Eunomius, particularly the restatement of their positions in popular Constantinopolitan society. Even these two strong examples will not demonstrate my thesis but they may offer some sense of its merits.

A look at Athanasius' writings shows that he both refers to the famous technical Greek terms of classical Trinitarian and Christological debate, *ousia, hypostasis* and *homoousios,* and that on occasion he attempts to explain their meanings.[1] He had been at the Council of Nicaea in 325, not as a bishop, but as a deacon, perhaps as a secretary to the bishop of Alexandria. You may remember that the word, *homoousios,* appears to have been the suggestion to Constantine of Hosius, his western theological advisor. Thus in one way this orthodox litmus test was placed prominently within the debate and even within the creed by a political figure like Constantine, who did not understand many of the issues, on the suggestion of Hosius, a western theologian who may not have understood a great deal more about the arguments than Constantine did. Political power called the council, paid for it and guided it. That should always make us uneasy. Yet the church has received this sense of Trinity and Christology and received it even in the midst of rejecting "Christendom."[2]

The deepest question, however, is what *homoousios,*"of the same substance or essence" was supposed to signify? It could be and probably was seen as a way to deny the claims of Arius that the Son was a secondary being whose divinity was derived from the Father, not a first-order being who from eternity was divine with the Father. Although Arius' works come to us in bits and pieces, he did seem to think of the Son's divinity as given to him through a participation by grace.[3] And he and his followers are said to have insisted that there was [a time before time began] when the Son did not exist.[4]

Arius was no great innovator; he was more an exegete and a popularizer of the faith than what we think of as a philosophical theologian. But he insisted on conserving an apophatic or negative theology he had inherited. God is one and totally beyond us, his creatures. We do not understand; God's thoughts are not our thoughts. God has made himself known in Jesus Christ, but for that purpose God created a secondary divine being who fit our thoughts, our world. If Arius developed a different twist it was in the realm of soteriology. According to him we will be saved by following Christ's example, trying to become like him, not because God became human that humans might become divine.[5]

Athanasius and the orthodox had to deal with a number of the philosophical issues involved. Their efforts were not as helpful as those which were to come later from the Cappadocians. Part of the reason was that in the early Arian debate a clear distinction between *ousia* and *hypostasis*, between essence or substance and individual person, was not created or invoked. *Homoousios* indicated that the Son and the Father shared the same essence, but that could be interpreted in ways that destroyed their distinct individual characteristics. In the case of Athanasius' view of Christology, his arguments were weakened by that fact that until 362, and perhaps beyond, he had little or no concern with the human soul of Jesus. He did not predicate any attitudes or actions of the human Jesus; everything about Jesus was attributed to the divine Word.

Much of this is best understood in the light of philosophical problems in the ancient world, particularly the way in which various theologians appropriated the positions of Platonic schools. Yet even within the period of these debates there are interesting clues about how hermeneutics and incarnation worked together in the task of making sense of Scripture. Athanasius' early tracts *Against the Heathen* and *The Incarnation of the Word*, written when he was in his twenties, show no signs of the Arian controversy. There is no discussion of Arius and no concern with the *homoousios*. Athanasius can talk about the Incarnation of Christ through biblical metaphors and models with great power and effectiveness, remarkable for someone of his age. He claims that God became man in order that humans might become divine.[6] But in the next few years the disagreements with Arius arose and the Council of Nicaea was called. From 325 on the battle only heated up. The apparent victory under Constantine shattered when Constantine exiled Athanasius for his continued struggle against the Arians; the next emperor supported the followers of Arius against the Nicenes. Athanasius fought hard to defend his position and found that each side played political hardball. Accused of having cut off a man's hand and used it in magical liturgies he defended himself by producing the fellow with both hands intact.[7] But that kind of attack and counter attack marked the controversy. During that period Athanasius more than once proposed *homoousios* as a key if not *the* key term in the debate, but even then he used the term primarily only in two treatises and then only within sections of them.[8]

In his sixties, still fighting the wars with the Arians which exacted their toll, Athanasius was asked by the monks with whom he was living to explain the problems of the Arian views: what are the basic issues? When he wrote his *Discourses against the Arians* he hardly mentioned the word *homoousios*. He refers to it only once and then in a confessional passage which recalls the Council of Nicaea. He seems confident that he can explain the mistakes of Arius and the proper understanding of the faith without discussing *homoousios*. The bulk of his attempt refers to Scripture.

Athanasius did not forego a discussion of *homoousios* because his side was definitely winning the contest and the aging leader could be magnanimous. He wrote the *Discourses* for a monastic community but he was in that community because the political authorities had sent him there in exile, the third of the five times he was forced out of Alexandria. As a battle hardened warrior, Athanasius might be expected to stay true to form. So the emotional vituperations of his opening lines should not shock. He personifies the Arian heresy as a she-devil attracting the insane and irreligious. She is the harbinger of the Anti-Christ, crafty and cunning like her father the Devil.

Even here the intriguing aspect of this description is that attention to the Bible is the significant point. This female devil, Arianism, is like her father in that she clothes her words in Scripture. As the Devil tempted Jesus with Scripture, so Arianism tempts its followers with Sacred Writ. Indeed one of the charges the Arians raise against the Nicenes is that Athanasius and his crowd use an unscriptural word, *homoousios*, as an important part of their position. Athanasius counters that *agennetos*, "unbegotten," used by Arians as the definitive name for God, is itself not a scriptural word, but one accepted from the philosophers; thus the Arians are not true to the principle they accuse the Nicenes of breaking.[9] In Athanasius' view the Arians' greatest failure with regard to what they teach is that they seem to use the Bible to defend their positions while they actually defame and destroy its truth. Within the ten introductory chapters of book one where Athanasius provides a general overview of Arius' teaching, he deals with Arius' positions from the vantage point of what we might call philosophical and systematic theology. Yet even there he refers again and again to Arius' problems in interpreting Scripture. Arius quotes passages which seem to support his positions but he takes no account of those verses which go against his views and thus does not give the whole view from the Bible. He misreads Paul. He asks questions not focused on Holy Writ but founded on the conundrums of the Greeks.[10]

If one takes the three books of the *Discourses against the Arians* as genuine,[11] then the bulk of the work is an attempt to explain the important biblical verses that are involved. The last three chapters of Book One and all of Book Two deal with the exegesis of scriptural passages: Philippians 2:9-10, Psalm 45:7-8, Hebrews 1:4, Hebrews 3:2, Acts 2:36, as well as a long seven-chapter discussion of Proverbs 8:22 and its context. Then Book Three counters with Nicene texts: John 14:10, 17:3, 6:38 and 14:28 in the context of God's claims to be one God in the Old Testament. John 10:30 and 17:11 also form part of this argument, but then Athanasius turns to verses in what we call the Synoptic Gospels to make the same claims. A whole swarm of Gospel texts is used to show that the Arian claim concerning Jesus Christ's secondary nature, a nature less than that of God the Father, is untrue.

The type of exegesis employed is not a distanced historical, grammatical study but a highly theological and polemical attempt. In more than one instance we well might call Athanasius to task for taking a text out of context, for pushing and pulling on a passage until it fits what he needs for his argument. That would be in line with various cogent observations made in recent years that Athanasius is not entirely fair in his representations of Arius' positions, that at times he draws inferences from Arius' positions that Arius may not have drawn.[12] But one of the impressions you do take away from this work is that theological exegesis is important for the church. Critical distance from the text is not all that nourishes believers. There must also be passionate involvement in the text, meditation upon its meaning. If Scripture says that the Son is God, a difficult, troubling truth for early Christians to see, then it is not inconsequential if someone else says he is not. None of us happily takes on the inquisitional history of the church as our history, but I doubt if anyone should be followed who insists that civility disallows claims for the divinity of Christ, none defended and none denied. Athanasius thinks the whole center of Christian faith is being dismantled by Arius. How can humans be saved if the fully divine Son of God did not become incarnate to save us? Why are we baptized into the Father, Son and Spirit if the Son and the Spirit are secondary deities or creatures? For Athanasius it is not possible to interpret Scripture without the theological setting of the church. A belief in one God, the sense that the incarnate fully-divine Son came to save us, and baptism into the name of the Father, Son and Holy Spirit provide a context for exegesis. And in Athanasius' view, that context squares with the claims of Scripture itself. When the Son is given such high titles and such divine actions, how can he not be God? He says "I and the Father are one" and "He who has seen me has seen the Father." It would not have occurred to Athanasius that the worshipping tradition of his church was at odds with the claims of Scripture. They were a working unity that was threatened by Arius' one-sidedness.

Thus Athanasius not only does not explain the *homoousios* very often, he also does not employ it as the main weapon in his attacks on Arius. His usual response concentrates on different questions. How can Arius teach what he does when the Gospel of John and other biblical passages say so many things that do not fit into his systematic, syllogistic theology? How can Arius teach what he does when Christian prayer and Christian baptism clearly assume the full divinity of Christ? *Homoousios* was not unimportant in the debates; indeed theology was not merely the restatement of Scripture and the recalling of worship. But much more than any of the histories of Christian doctrine ever indicate, worship and Holy Writ formed the positions hammered out by those fathers whom we now consider orthodox, catholic, and biblical.

The Cappadocian fathers, Basil of Caesarea, Gregory of Nyssa and Gregory of Nazianzus, are credited with having created the necessary linguistic and conceptual distinctions that define particularly the Trinitarian solution of the fourth century church and strongly preview the Christological solution of the fifth century church. An epistle probably written by Gregory of Nyssa, Basil of Caesarea's brother, also appears in the corpus of Basil's letters.[13] Most contemporary scholars think that Nyssa had the more philosophical turn of mind and thus attribute the epistle to him.[14] It is true that the letter carefully distinguishes between the levels of oneness and plurality within the Trinity. It claims that *ousia*, "essence" or "nature" should be used for the shared oneness of Father, Son and Spirit; *hypostasis*, "person or individual entity" should be used for the particular characteristics of each one. Thus the Nicene claim that the Son is *homoousios* with the Father is given a deeper philosophical definition than that provided by Athanasius who had not seen how to distinguish *ousia* and *hypostasis* in these ways. The distinctions depend upon subtle philosophical thought as many scholars have shown, but as important for our interests here, the epistle itself insists that such a differentiation is demanded by what Scripture says, not singularly what philosophy demands.[15] The wide knowledge of holy writ which these brothers brought to their task of contextualization was in their view the driving force behind the need to employ the consistent use of the philosophical terms.

Gregory of Nazianzus, the third of the Cappadocians, is considered by Eastern Orthodoxy to be one of the three hierarchs of the faith, along with Basil of Caesarea and John Chrysostom. Yet contemporary surveys often describe him as the least gifted theologian of the Cappadocians even though Eastern Orthodoxy calls him the Theologian, a title that tradition also gives only to the Apostle John. That should be some kind of clue that Eastern Orthodoxy seldom sees the task of theology in the same way that we who are trained within the Enlightenment influenced West have viewed it.

Gregory was a sensitive leader, one worth getting to know, but his works do not meet the criteria of what some see as the task of a theologian because he does not produce long explanations of ever more tightly defined theological terms or formulas. He says that the best theologians are poet-philosophers, ones who have meditated day and night on the truths of the faith and can offer clearer images to those who know that images are all we can see in this glass darkly. Nazianzen put together a series of five sermons attacking the Arian understanding of Trinity and Christology, but how he did it is interesting. He was in a bind. The Neo-Arian leaders, his opponents, were often men of high education and learning, particularly in various philosophical schools. They accused him of being a country bumpkin, someone who had grown up in a small town, who wasn't much to look at and had a funny accent. He hadn't grown up in great Constantinople where he was then preaching; he conceded that he would win no beauty pageants; he agreed that he had a provincial accent.[16]

But he had received one of the best educations that the ancient world could provide; eventually he had studied at Alexandria and Athens, the finest "universities" of his day. So he could take on the philosophical moves of his opponents and did. For someone like me who loves philosophy he is an interesting character. But his five theological orations are set within much larger concerns than the philosophical situation.[17] He begins with an appeal that the Arians do not know what a theologian should be. They love to talk about theology in the most inappropriate places: on street corners, at feasts and funerals, in women's salons.[18] Gregory of Nyssa also noted that such conversation of Trinitarian theology was to be heard in banks, groceries and the baths.[19] Those observations can be read in at least two ways. First, both Gregories felt that talk about theology should be seriously considered in the midst of worship; theology was for and from the church. But, second, it is also clear that the apparent discussion of *homoiousios* and *homoousios* was not always in terms of the most learned philosophers or theologians. Theology was an important topic for people; they might talk about it nearly anywhere. Thus sermons given within churches evidently dealt with themes that interested the populace, particularly more well-to-do folk who had time for such talk.

In Gregory Nazianzen's view the Arians do not know how difficult it is to speak well about the deep things of God. They encourage young adults to act as experts on the subject when in reality it takes maturity, indeed many years of deep prayer and meditation to talk about such topics.[20]

In his second oration he points out that finally, God's nature, what God's very being is, cannot be known by human beings. Somewhat like Arius, and quite unlike Aetius and Eunomius, Nazianzen insists that we cannot know the deepest things about the nature of divinity. Our minds are just too tiny as instruments to encompass all that God is. It is not that we merely have trouble getting the right words to explain God; we cannot get the right thoughts, the proper concepts.[21] Elsewhere in these five orations he warns that we often make stupid mistakes by thinking that the gender of a scriptural word means it is masculine or feminine. Thus some might be misled to think that God is male when in fact God is neither male nor female in our sense of those terms.[22] In the end God's nature is incomprehensible; we know enough about God to follow but never as much about God as God knows. Gregory chides the Arians for thinking that they can understand so much about God's nature when there is so much about their own being and wider nature that they do not know. Although we might be able to answer some of the questions he raises: what makes the rivers run to the seas and the seas stay contained, etc., we have other puzzles that should also make us humble. The Theologian finally ridicules the Arians for thinking that they know all the intricacies of God's nature, what its name is, what it can and cannot be, when they so clearly are ignorant of many things about themselves and their world.

Quite unlike Arius, and differently from Aetius and Eunomius, Gregory insists that apophatic or negative theology is not an end in itself. Of course we cannot know everything about God. But one of the reasons for the Son's incarnation was to teach us the character of God sufficiently that we could know God's main purpose. God incarnate in Christ keeps us from always having to answer the question, "what is two times five?", with answers like, "Not six or seven or eleven or fourteen." Sometimes we can just say "Ten." Jesus Christ allows us to utter such things about God so that our theology is both apophatic and kataphatic; much it cannot answer, but some of the most important questions it can answer sufficiently.

When Nazianzen turns in theological Orations Three and Four to the Trinitarian and Christological issues, he does not leave his deep sense of humility or his understanding that theologians must be meditative poets. Neither does he leave his philosophical attack behind. But his main consideration is what Scripture itself says and what the church in its worship has been doing. Worship is not mentioned as frequently as some other observations but it is decisive. If you pray to Christ how can you say that he is not divine as the Father is divine? What would be the point of your prayer if you think him a secondary figure? Why does the church baptize you in the name of the Father and the Son and the Spirit if they do not share a common divinity? Are you baptized in the name of creatures?

It is wrong to assume that all his Neo-Arian opponents were philosophers who required only a strict logic for their theology. Aetius' *Syntagmation* contains very tight formulations. Eunomius has a strong philosophical interest and did use some of the more interesting developments in philosophy to back up his claims,[23] but he also wrote a commentary on Romans. Nazianzen probably knew their works; at least he knew people in Constantinople who had been influenced by their teaching. Yet recent research has established clearly that Neo-Arians as well as early Arians were worshipping Christians who had their own sense of what the faith was.[24] Some Arians may have baptized with only one immersion rather than the three so often used in orthodox congregations; they may have baptized believers only into the death of Christ.[25] Arians were concerned with worship and did use poetic language in their liturgies, even to the point of speaking of the death of Christ as the passion of the impassible one, the corruption of the incorruptible one so that our state might be changed to incorruptibility, phrases also uttered by the orthodox.[26] Perhaps if Arians and Nicenes had found ways to worship together they could have discovered and emphasized some of the similarities that might have overcome their differences. But by the time that Nazianzen had reached Constantinople, viciousness had arisen between the two groups. For decades Nicene emperors had driven Arian bishops out and Arian emperors had driven Nicene bishops out. Gregory claims that Arian rabble had attacked his congregation while they were worshipping, even killing some people in the sanctuary.[27] Shared worship had ceased.

The bulk of the Nazianzen's orations on the Son, however, are not concerned primarily with philosophy but with the interpretation of Holy Writ. The point of Gregory's efforts is that the Arians do funny things with Scripture. They define the nature of the Father, Son and Holy Spirit specifically from a philosophical doctrine of names and then they select biblical passages to support their views. They might have done it the other way round; they might have read some passages and gotten their idea of selecting particular philosophical arguments to illustrate those views, but in either case they have made disastrous mistakes. By selecting only a few verses and then neglecting others they do not present the whole scriptural picture of Jesus the Christ.

In the next oration Gregory assembles a group of biblical texts which the Neo-

Arians seem to ignore, many taken from the Gospel of John. These texts not only imply but claim that the Son shares the divinity of the Father. The Theologian's final point is that when the largest group of scriptural texts is assembled which speak of Jesus Christ, his three fold model of predication: the Son before incarnation, the Son incarnate, and Jesus the man, is the interpretive framework which is most appropriate. The Arian framework of a less than fully divine Son with no human mind or will does not do justice to the breadth and depth of scriptural claims.

The Theologian also collected a list of passages which the Neo-Arians interpreted as basic to their position that Christ is a creature and not divine like God the Father. He goes through ten clusters of texts and shows how his interpretive models, his Christological principles, can make sense of those passages. Some verses must refer to the Son before his incarnation; others must refer to the Son incarnate when he was subject to human limitations in many ways; still others must refer to the full humanity of Jesus, his intellect and his will. In that way none of the passages about weakness or lack of knowledge need be used to prove that the Son is not divine like God the Father. It is either the Son limited by his incarnate condition or Jesus in his full humanity that is the subject of those verses. Yet for Gregory these exegetical distinctions did not mean that Christ was many subjects in the sense that he was no longer one person. Together these hermeneutical models allow the Theologian to cite over four hundred passages of Scripture in the two orations devoted to Christology.[28]

As a rule Nazianzen's exegesis is grammatical and theological. R.P.C. Hanson, in his last and perhaps greatest book, insisted that there is more common sense in Gregory's exegesis than can be found in any other of the fathers.[29] Nazianzen reads the texts with the full sense brought to him by his rhetorical education. Like both grammarians and linguistic, analytic philosophers he finds the meaning of words in their contexts rather than in some root definition which they carry into each sentence.[30] He continually warns his opponents that they have not paid close enough attention to what is actually said or the context in which it is said.

We learn some interesting aspects of his Christology as he works within those rules. Commenting on John 6:38 the Theologian says that if the verse were concerned with Jesus' human nature which is like ours we would not be at all surprised that Jesus said he came not to do his own will but the will of the father. All humans have a will that can resist God. But the context says that it is the will of him who came down, so the passage speaks of Jesus Christ's divine will. Yet the cry from the cross and the agony of Gethsemane belong to the man Jesus.[31] In careful interpretive comments like these Gregory prefigures the sense of later councils that Jesus had not only a divine will but a fully human will. In other passages he predicates attitudes and actions of both the divine Son and the full humanity so that, beyond the insight which Athanasius had, Nazianzen provides a Christology that precedes Chalcedon and yet insists that Jesus Christ is one person in two natures, not one person out of two natures in the sense that after the birth of Christ there was only one divine nature.

Having looked at these early Christian leaders in terms of what the bulk of their writings indicate has, I trust, been helpful. They knew so much Scripture and found so much of it in need of some kind of unifying hermeneutical principles and confessional statements that they created what we might call the legacy of patristic theology. The payoff from this kind of survey is, I hope, clear. First, Trinitarian and Christological confessions are primarily hermeneutical models. The Cappadocians, particularly Gregory Nazianzen, understood that their technical terms only provided illustrations or shadows of the truth; today we might refer to them as heuristic tools.[32] They thought that their models not only allowed but promoted the saturation of the Christian community with Scripture; they claimed that people saturated in Holy Writ would find their theological views helpful in making sense of all the Bible. If you know what is said in so many biblical passages about Jesus' ignorance, weakness, etc. you have a difficult time not thinking of him as a human person. But if you also know what Scripture says about his miracles, his knowledge of other people's thoughts, his claims concerning his oneness with God the Father, you have little difficulty thinking of him as divine. In our era classical conservative formulas have often demeaned his humanity; classical liberal formulas dismissed his divinity. Yet something tells you that a Jesus with multiple personalities in one body makes him a freak rather than a whole person we should follow. And if he is divine like God the Father, and the Spirit is divine, then there is a Trinitarian claim as well.

It is not, however, an option to drop the Nicene and Chalcedonian confessions from five thousand feet and know their impact will be constructive.[33] Neither do the present theological dust storms about doing away with the old, meaningless language in order to fit our present pluralistic age offer much but blinding effects. We all know that leaving Trinitarian language behind would immediately change our conversations with Jews and Muslims. Both missiologists and up-to-date modern, northern hemisphere theologians can see the point of that. But our question must be, how Hellenized and thus expendable are the ancient confessions? If we take them away and try to read the Bible with some understanding of who Jesus is, what will we say? Is he a good guy? Or is the New Testament trying to tell us that this fellow is more than a man, more than a second-rank divinity? He is God in the flesh. If we are to allow no divine claims about Jesus, we not only have to be modern or carefully pluralistic; we also have to mute, change or do away with many texts of Holy Writ that have caused the Trinitarian and Christological queries to be raised.

Presently most Christian traditions known to me are trying with some success to reintroduce Scripture reading and study into their local congregations. If knowledge of the Bible is what brings up the questions that the ancient theologians tried to answer with their apparently old, tired formulas and hermeneutical principles, why would we seek to do away with their efforts just now? Their solutions should be guides to help us find some kinds of answers for our own situation. I am not interested in deleting the *homoousios* from the Nicene and Nicene-Constantinopolitan creed because it has philosophical and traditional overtones, is not a word from Scripture, and was both suggested and enforced through imperial political power. If we all pay attention to what the missiologists call contextualization, the attempt to state the gospel within a culture in such a way that it speaks to those in that culture, we can see how important this strange word and its counterparts *ousia* and *hypostasis* were and are. They allowed the church to speak in shorthand about what it considered to be the significant biblical truth found within its sense of worship: The Christ is God—not a secondary being or a second hand deity, but truly God. But when we confess the *homoousios*, perhaps in some newer translation as "one in being with the Father," we must not forget how the early leaders got to that. I am not a New Testament specialist, but it still amazes me that in the sixth decade of the first century C.E., probably earlier, Hellenized Jewish Christians could sing the hymns of Philippians 2 and Colossians 1 which the apostle Paul uses. It is no less remarkable to me that near the end of the century the apostle John could write his prologue and have

Thomas declare when he saw the risen Christ, "My Lord and my God." Those few verses, so often debated, do not establish without a doubt that the earliest Christians saw Christ as *homoousios*, "one in being with the Father." But when I think particularly of the Jewish influence on early Christianity I sense the struggle it was for them to create those early hymns and what it must have taken for the writer of John to pen that prologue. I tend to find it entering into the unfathomable when Hans Küng compares the claims for divinity that grew up around the figure of Gautama Buddha over a period of five hundred years, with the hymns that early Jewish Christians sang within one or two decades of Jesus' death and find the claims and the process to be about the same.[34]

A significant part of the classical Christological debates concerned the interpretation of the Bible. The positions which we now call "orthodox" commend themselves to us because they deal more fairly with more Scripture. Within technical patristic studies, however, the Arians and Neo-Arians have been getting much of the play in recent years and that not unfairly. Yet to put the connections plainly, it is not accidental that Maurice Wiles has been a force not only in helping us see the positions of Arius, Asterius and Eunomius more clearly at the same time that he has been one of the leaders of the *Myth of God Incarnate* debate.[35] Much like the Arians of old he does not think that any of us can make much sense of so-called "orthodox" talk about God incarnate. His essays in the *Myth of God Incarnate* are filled with philosophical power and insight, but they do not strike me as full enough of the various scriptural insights that figures like Athanasius and Gregory found. My attempt is not to tar him with the brush of an old heresy, but to suggest that his efforts to refurbish the theologies of Arius, Asterius and Eunomius are directly connected to his claims in the *Myth of God Incarnate* debate although at times in very complex ways.

My point is simple. I am not at all convinced that careful, sensible, grammatical and contextual exegesis of New Testament passages about Jesus Christ will lead one to abandon the ancient creeds. I do not think that the Incarnation is a mythical structure that should be discarded by modern folk. Yet we cannot use fourth and fifth century confessions without placing them within our own contexts. In a marvelous little book entitled *Truly a Person, Truly God*, Adrian Thatcher has suggested on the basis of analytical philosophy, particularly the personality theory developed in that philosophy by P. F. Strawson and others, that the old formula, one person in two natures, needs attention.[36] The truth of the old confession is best preserved in our era by saying that Jesus was truly a human person and at the same time that he was truly God. Personality theory has shown how much mystery, how much wonder, is involved in human personality, an insight which we who trust a God whose ways are far beyond our ways should claim. In order to keep in place within our own twentieth century northern hemisphere cultures (and probably southern hemisphere cultures also) what the fourth and fifth century churches confessed, we need to confess—that Jesus was a real human person with limitations and temptations and yet was also truly God. Here is a suggestion of a hermeneutical model that takes cognizance of much Scripture and earlier tradition while concentrating on how we can use intellectual insights of our own era to express the ancient truths. It once again combines wonder, worship and writ.

When we think about the efforts of first century and fourth century Christian communities, we must turn again to the sense of contextualization and ask what they were trying to bring into their cultures through the words they chose to employ. That is a tale for another time, but at least I can ask whether the Arian and Neo-Arian attempts at contextualization of the gospel were as true to the wholeness of Scripture as were those of Athanasius and Gregory. If you know that your Christology needs to be put into the language of the street, the words of your culture, so that it can appeal to those who live in your region, what will you say? I think that once we know that it is impossible to be totally objective, we need to find our character, our teaching, our life within the community of Christians, not in some nonexistent unbiased public square which sets all the rules. And when we look to those Christian communities for our cues, we will find Scripture playing an important role in each of them. As we look to the Bible we will find that there is a need for organizing models to express the central message. Arius, Aetius and Eunomius thought that the various passages of Scripture which spoke of the limitations of Christ demanded that his divinity be viewed as less than that of the Father. They posited one controlling subject, the divine Son. And since that Son had obvious limits, he could not share the same being with the Father.

But Athanasius and especially Gregory suggested other hermeneutical models for dealing with a fuller array of verses from Holy Writ. If a reader of Scripture heard Peter say that God has made this Jesus both Lord and Christ, if she listened when John has Jesus say, "The Father is greater than I," if he heard Colossians saying that Christ was the first born of all creation, weren't these people to understand that the Son was less than the Father. But what were those readers or listeners to understand when Philippians said that Christ Jesus did not count equality with God as something to be grasped, but emptied himself and took on the form of a servant? What were they to hear when John said the Word was God and Thomas confessed that the risen Jesus was his Lord and his God. What does Colossians mean when it says that "in him the fullness of the Godhead dwelt bodily"?

The Christology of Athanasius insisted that the divinity of Jesus was the same as that of the Father. He hammered away at what he saw to be an Arian penchant for taking some of Holy Writ and making it basic while not attending to other passages. Yet Athanasius' hermeneutical model was flawed because he did not allow the humanity of Jesus to be in any way the subject of verses in Scripture. It was the Cappadocians, particularly Gregory of Nazianzus, who not only pressed for talking about the oneness and threeness of the Trinity on different levels, but also insisted that talk about Jesus demanded double or triple predication. For Nazianzen there were three possible subjects for any biblical passage about Jesus Christ: the Son in his unlimited divine capacity before the Incarnation, the Son in his divine capacity limited during the Incarnation, and the man Jesus in his limited human capacity. Gregory did not make these hermeneutical insights hard and fast rules. Thus he did not divide the incarnate Christ into two sons, one human and one divine. His sense of worship and mystery led him to speak of the passion of the impassible Son, to insist the human and divine had interpenetrated each other so that there was one person in two natures. In ways that I always admire he worked hard to clarify how we should read the scriptural verses about Jesus at the same time that we did not make our confession of who he was and is into a finicking little formula that tied up all the loose ends. We are the ones at loose ends; as humans, even redeemed humans, we will never understand fully, perhaps not even in heaven.[37] Our lives here and there will be filled with wonder.

NOTES

1. Athanasius, *Epistle to Serapion* and *Concerning the Synod.*

2. See particularly the articles by John Meyendorff, André Halleux and A. James Reimer in *Faith to Creed: Ecumenical Perspectives on the Affirmation of the Apostolic Faith in the Fourth Century,* ed. by S. Mark Heim, "Faith and Order/USA" (Grand Rapids, MI: Wm. B. Eerdmans, 1991).

3. Athanasius *Discourses against the Arians* I,2,6 and I,3,9 appears to quote that phrase from Arius' *Thalia.*

4. The phrase translated "there was when he was not" is perhaps the most famous of all the lines said to have come from Arius. It stays within the debate well into the fifth century, after most Arians have disappeared. There seems to be little reason to doubt that it was a major claim of that group. See *Discourses Against the Arians* I,4, *passim.*

5. The literature on early Arianism has become so large that it is nearly unmanageable. Two works in English commend themselves: Rowan Williams, *Arius: Heresy and Tradition* (London: Darton, Longman and Todd, 1987) is magisterial. Robert Gregg and Dennis Groh, *Early Arianism: A View of Salvation* (Philadelphia: Fortress Press, 1981) is insightful in insisting that soteriology was the center of the debate, but unbalanced because it does not notice the importance of monotheism for that debate.

6. *On the Incarnation* 4, 11, 16, 22 and especially 54.

7. The supposed hand of Arsenius was produced at the Tyre council. But Sozomen *H.E.* 2,25 notes that Athanasius' accusers claimed to think that Arsenius was dead. Socrates *H.E.* 1,27 says they knew he was alive for they had hid him away. Duane Wade-Hampton Arnold, *The Early Episcopal Career of Athanasius of Alexandria* (Notre Dame, IN: University of Notre Dame Press, 1991) warns that Athanasius was not the ruthless politician which the charges at the Synod of Tyre accused him of being.

8. Athanasius, *Epistle to Serapion* and *Concerning the Synod.*

9. *Discourses Against the Arians* I, 9

10. *Discourses against the Arians* I, 1, 3, 4, 6, 7, 9.

11. The Fourth Book has long been seen as by some other author, perhaps Didymus the Blind or Apollinaris. Its vocabulary and thought are quite different from that of Athanasius. There is a contemporary debate about whether the Third Book is genuinely Athanasian. The accepted view is that it is authentic; Charles Kannangiesser, *Athanase d'Alexandrie évêque et écrivain: une lecture des traités Contra les Ariens* (Paris: Becauchesne, 1983) [for a summary in English see "Athanasius of Alexandria: Three Orations Against the Arians, a Reappraisal," *Studia Patristica* 18 (1982) 981-995] has given much time and energy to proving that it is not. As yet his case has not been fully accepted. But if it were to reach that status it would only strengthen the thesis I am defending here: that much of the Arian debate was about Scripture and its meaning, indeed that was the crux of the issues raised. For Kannengiesser's case depends in large part on his observations that the terminology used in Book Three is more philosophical and less biblical than the language used in the first two books. I am not yet fully convinced because it seems in line with the plan of the work that Athanasius would have wanted to exegete the scriptural passages that supported his view of Trinity and Christology. Those passages are discussed in Book Three. But in either case the importance of hermeneutics and biblical exegesis looms large in the arguments.

12. See particularly Stuart G. Hall, "The *Thalia* of Arius in Athanasius' Accounts," *Arianism:*

Historical and Theological Reassessments, Papers from the Ninth International Conference on Patristic Studies, Oxford, September -10, 1983, Patristic Monograph Series, 11 (Cambridge, MA: The Philadelphia Patristic Foundation, Ltd., 1985) 37-58.

13. *Saint Basil, the Letters*, ed, and trans. by Roy Deferrari, "The Loeb Classical Library," (Cambridge, MA: Harvard University Press, 1972) I, Ep. 38.

14. Johannes Quasten, *Patrology*, (Utrecht: Spectrum Publishers, 1966) III, 281.

15. *Ep*. 38, Loeb edition, 204, 218.

16. *Or*. 33, 6-8.

17. See *Faith Gives Fullness to Reasoning : The Five Theological Orations of Gregory Nazianzen*, introduction and commentary by Frederick Norris, translation by Lionel Wickham and Frederick Williams, "Supplements to *Vigiliae Christianae*, Vol. XIII" (Leiden: E.J. Brill, 1991).

18. *Or*. 27, 2. It is difficult to tell how deeply sexist the last phrase was. Nazianzen as a monk held strong ascetic views. The violation of the woman's chamber was important to him. He also had great affection for both his mother, Nonna, and his sister, Gorgonia; he wrote a beautiful oration for each on the occasion of her death. To him they were models of virtue. But they were not given the opportunities for education that he used even though the family had great wealth.

19. Gregory of Nyssa in his *De Deitate Filii et Spiritus Sancti PG* 46, 557

20. *Or*. 27, 1-9.

21. *Or*. 28, 4. He warns that Plato was wrong in suggesting that he knew but could not say what that reality was. No human knows.

22. *Or*. 31, 7.

23. Raoul Mortley, *From Word to Silence: The Way of Negation, Christian and Greek*, 2 vols. "Theophaneia, Vol. 31" (Bonn, 1986) shows how much the Neo-Arians astutely used new philosophical advances in their arguments.

24. See particularly Thomas Kopecek, "Neo-Arian Religion: The Evidence of the *Apostolic Constitutions*," *Arianism: Historical and Theological Reassessments* 153-179.

25. Socrates *H.E.* 5.24; Sozomen *H.E.* 6.26; The seventh canon of the 381 Council of Constantinople.

26. The evidence comes from Latin-speaking Arians, but it is quite interesting. See Fr. 20, p. 260 in R. Gryson, *Scripta Arriana Latina*, "Corpus Christianorum Series Latina," LXXXVII (Turnhout: Brepols, 1982).

27. *Or*. 33, 3-4.

28. *Ors*. 29 & 30.

29. R.P.C. Hanson, *The Search for the Christian Doctrine of God: The Arian Controversy 318-381* (Edinburgh: T & T Clark, 1988) 846.

30. See my forthcoming article, "Theology as Grammar: bregory Nazianzen and Ludwig Wittgenstein," *Arianism after Arius*, ed. by Michel Barnes and Daniel H. Williams (Edinburgh: T. & T. Clark, 1992).

31. *Or*. 30,12.

32. *Ep*. 38, anciently attributed to both Basil and Gregory of Nyssa, probably does belong to Nyssa. But this most technical piece from the Cappadocians, which distinguishes *ousia* and *hypostasis*, also notes that its words are only "illustrations" and "shadows," *hypodeigma* and *skia*. See the Loeb edition, 212. Gregory the Theologian, *Or*. 31,31-33, notices that he has tried to find good illustrations in the world for the doctrine of the Trinity, but each one has weaknesses. These theologians never saw their words and phrases as necessary for encapsuling reality. That was the mistake they charged the Neo-Arians with making.

33. Nicholas Lash, *Change in Focus: A Study in Doctrinal Change and Continuity* (London: Sheed and Ward, 1973) 147 notes that "doctrines, rites or institutions" when "simply carried over, 'untranslated' become not merely useless, but harmful. In the new context they do not, and cannot, express the *same* meanings as they originally did."

34. Hans Küng *et al.*, *Christianity and the World Religions: Paths to Dialogue with Islam, Hinduism and Buddhism*, trans. by Peter Heinegg (Garden City, NY Doubleday, 1986). See the papers of

Wright and Marshall in this volume for the early claims about Jesus.

35. Maurice Wiles, "Christianity without Incarnation?" and "Myth in Theology," *The Myth of God Incarnate*, ed. by John Hick (Philadelphia: The Westminster Press, 1977) 1-10 and 148-166. Also see his "Asterius: A New Chapter in the History of Arianism," in collaboration with Robert Gregg, *Arianism: Historical and Theological Assessments*, 111-151 and "Eunomius: hair-splitting dialectician or defender of the accessibility of salvation?" *The making of orthodoxy: Essays in honour of Henry Chadwick*, ed. by Rowan Williams (Cambridge: Cambridge University Press, 1989) 157-172. The exposition of Asterius' homilies concludes that early Arianism was "a movement, however misguided, of a religious and evangelical spirit, a movement whose heart and basic motivation was a passionate defence of the gospel of the incarnation," 140 The positive assessment of Eunomius notes that Wiles is not calling for "a reversal of the judgment made in favour of Cappadocian orthodoxy" 169.

36. Adrian Thatcher, *Truly a Person, Truly God: A Post-Mythical View of Jesus* (London: SPCK, 1990). Also see George Lindbeck's discussion of Nicaea and Chalcedon in *The Nature of Doctrine: Religion and Theology in a Postliberal Age* (Philadelphia: The Westminster Press, 1984) 92-96.

37. *Or*. 27, 10, the final poetic confession.

AFRICAN AMERICAN CHRISTIAN PERSPECTIVES ON CHRISTOLOGY AND INCARNATION

LARRY MURPHY

The intention of this paper is to present an historical overview of the particular perspectives of African American Christians on the topics of Christology and Incarnation. Pastors and theological faculty can probably recall from the receding memories of their seminary training the traditional Christological formulations of the Church dealing with Christ as the second person of the Trinity, *homoousion* rather than *homoiousion*—of the same substance, rather than of like substance with the Creator ("Father"). They might recall debates involving such persons as Athanasius, Appolinaris, Cyril, and Nestorius over the relationship of the divine and the human in Christ. The prevailing consensus emerging in the West was that Jesus was "wholly God and fully human ('man')." But pronouncements such as these represent, in large measure, the Christ of Western doctrinal and systematic theology. I'm not sure that this Christ has ever been appropriated into the operative, personal faith affirmations of common Christians through the centuries. It certainly has not been the case for black Christians.

Who is Jesus the Christ? Black Christians characteristically have answered this question in functional terms, i.e., Jesus has been defined on the basis of how he has functioned in their lives, this experiential dimension being informed by the witness of Scripture and of human history.

I. THE BIBLE AND BLACK CHRISTIANS

Black Protestants share fully in the Protestant tradition of *word*-centered faith and worship. The Bible has been for them *the* book, the authority. Celebrity and authority in the preaching arena have come in proportion to one's ability to expound the Word with art, insight, and assuring relevance. And while black Christians have looked for a message supportive of their existence, for a sermon to be acceptable it has had to be drawn clearly from Scripture. For the Bible has been seen as the locus of salvific hope, the source of affirmation of black being against the existential onslaught of the society.

And so it was that the illiterate black slaves learned the Scriptures not by sight but by *heart* as they heard them read in the plantation devotional services or in Sunday worship. The intense desire for literacy found among so many slaves was based on the desire to be able to read the Scriptures for themselves. This spilled over in the post-Civil

War years into the establishment of hundreds of schools by and for blacks. Ninety-year-old emancipated grandparents sat in classrooms with their nine-year-old descendants, learning their ABC's so they could read of the "mighty acts of God" with their own eyes. It is an interesting historical note that the public educational system in the South came into existence largely from black initiative based on a desire for education to facilitate Christian nurture, as well as social advancement.

Black Christians have accepted the whole corpus of Scripture as the authoritative Word of God, giving no priority to either the Old or the New Testament. They have extracted and mingled didactic and illustrative materials from both in any given sermon, Sunday School lesson, etc. Yet, they have been far from indiscriminate in their use of Scripture. There has been an affinity for biblical narratives which highlight God's exercise of power and deliverance. And there has been a sense of identification with stories of persons who endured, in faith, against overwhelming odds. On the other hand, there has been much attention to those Scriptures which speak of love, whether between God and humans or between persons. Perhaps this reflected the yearning of a people rejected—" "rebuked and scorned," in the words of a Negro Spiritual—the yearning for the experience of love and acceptance in the world. In keeping with this, among many blacks in the past, the writings of Paul fell into disfavor, since certain passages from this author were offered regularly by whites as support for the social *status quo*, including slavery. Paul's works are generally acceptable today, however, now that they are not commonly appealed to for public justification of black oppression.

Now the starting point for hermeneutics in the black church has been that God is an omnipotent, benevolent, loving God who cares for the weak, the lowly, the downtrodden; God breaks oppression and delivers the enchained; God punishes evil and rewards righteousness. And though God's methods and plans may be above our comprehension, God's way is good and will ultimately prevail. The will of God is understood to be consistent with common sense and with the pragmatics of survival, including the survival needs of the oppressed.

These statements represent the givens, in the light of which blacks have understood all of Scripture. Black Christian theology, from colonial days to the present, reflects this; from Phyllis Wheatley and Richard Allen to Henry Garnett; from Nat Turner to Henry McNeal Turner; from Henry and Ella Mitchell to James Cone. A speech by a prominent nineteenth century black minister, the Rev. Nathaniel Paul, will serve to illustrate this point. In the speech, the Rev. Paul says that did he believe God were so cruel and unjust as to allow black enslavement to continue indefinitely, then he (Rev. Paul) would revile the church, burn his Bible as a book of falsehoods and fables, and reject the notion of God altogether. But Paul's ideas about God were not cognitive theories; they were faith convictions through the prism of which all other realities, including Scripture, must be viewed. Hence, no matter how firmly entrenched and enduring oppression might *seem* to be, its doom was nonetheless sure. Its tenacity was, at most, a challenge to the faithful to understand or accept God's timetable for action. In the Rev. Paul's words:

> The progress of emancipation, though slow, is nevertheless certain: it is certain because that God who has made of one blood all nations of men, and who is said to be no respecter of persons, has so decreed.[1]

Yet, some distinctions need to be made here, for within the context of the above givens, two different hermeneutical principles have generally been employed among black Christians: the typological and the Christological.[2] The former principle focuses upon God's acts within history, as related in Scripture, seeing them as prefigurations or types of what shall be repeated when the hour demands. So, for example, the acts of God in the exodus, in Daniel's safekeeping, and in Shadrach, Meshach, and Abednego's deliverance are taken as types of God's continuing action in history, of what God can be *relied upon* to do again and again. Witness the words of one Spiritual: "The God dat lived in Daniel's time is still the same today." The central concern here clearly is liberation and social transformation. The typological hermeneutical principle has been employed by some slave preachers, slave revolt leaders, and nineteenth and twentieth century social activists, who have been grasped by the liberationist aspects of their understanding of God.

The second principle, the Christological, focuses upon the spiritual work of Christ in the world, seeing that work foretold and anticipated in Old Testament times. For instance, the Old Testament messiah and Suffering Servant figures are taken as references to Christ. The concern underlying the Christological principle is the regeneration and salvation of individuals—securing a place in God's eternal realm. Among both slave and free black preachers, pre- and post-Civil War, the Christological was the more prominently employed interpretive principle.

These two hermeneutical principles have always been operative side by side in the black church, varying in their relative appeal with time and circumstance. For instance, Richard Allen in one published address warned whites that, by Scripture's witness, God characteristically casts down kings and nations for oppression—the typological. In a companion address to blacks, he admonished them to maintain exemplary Christian behavior, even at the cost of continual bondage, so that they might not forfeit the eternal salvation extended through Christ—the Christological.[3] In point of fact, black Christians have always held these two principles in tension within themselves, the one never intended to exclude the other.

The bridge that connected these two points and provided intercourse between them has been black Christians' understanding of the unity of the Godhead. The Christ of Bethlehem is believed to have been actively present in the acts of God in the Old Testament. For instance, this writer has heard black preachers identify the person discovered to be accompanying Shadrach, Meshach, and Abednego in the fiery furnace as Jesus the Christ (cf. Daniel 3:24-25). And so, black Christians have accepted that in the unity of the Godhead, the Creator acts with and through the Son/the Christ to effect temporal/historical deliverance, as well as eternal salvation. The typological and the Christological ends seemingly have been viewed as complementary dimensions of a single, uniform divine will, in the totality of which the Christ participates. The former is but a particularization in time of the universal divine love and justice which the latter conclusively signifies.

Black people in English North America began to be brought into the faith in earnest in the eighteenth and nineteenth centuries, primarily under the auspices of Evangelical Protestantism, with its focus on experiential piety. Black Christianity has continued to reflect these historical roots, while also being contextualized in a social location of oppression and marginalization. It is against this backdrop, with the unique religious insights it has afforded, that black Christians have responded to the Christological question. In order to see the spectrum and the nuances of the answers that have been given, I would like for us to look at three bodies of material: the Negro Spirituals; contemporary black devotional literature; and the writings and public pronouncements of twentieth century black theologians, professional and lay.

II. THE SPIRITUALS

The first notable thing about the Spirituals is that there are practically none which treat the Christmas event, the Incarnation. There is one which exclaims "Mary Had A Baby, Yes, Lord" and another which asks, "Oh, Mary, what you gonna call that pretty little baby?" Still another one heralds the Star in the East on Christmas morn and bids the shepherds to rise up and follow. The Incarnation is simply not represented as a pivotal event in salvation history.

James Weldon Johnson, noted student of the Negro Spirituals, surmises that the absence of the Christmas theme in this musical literature may be due to the low regard in which Christmas was held generally in the slave era South. He says the holiday was celebrated as a secular, even profane occasion of drinking and rowdiness. Slaves were encouraged to celebrate in like manner, being provided with ample food, alcoholic beverages, and temporarily increased liberties. In this atmosphere, says Johnson, ". . . there was destroyed in the minds of the slaves any connection between the birth of Christ and his life and death."[4]

Perhaps another explanation for the scant attention to Christ's birth in the Spirituals is the incomplete religious instruction afforded to slaves. Slaves tended to be taught those aspects of Scripture and Christian belief which their owners and clergy mentors believed to be consistent with their permanent status as chattel servants. The values of subservience, loyalty, and docility were the focus, rather than the fine points of doctrine. Still, one might have expected that slaves, persons of humble circumstances, would have built upon the parallels to Christ's meagre, harsh beginnings.

The crucifixion and resurrection of Christ, on the other hand, find much wider treatment in the Spirituals. Note such familiar titles as "Were You There?"; "He Never Said A Mumblin' Word"; "Do, Lord, Remember Me"; "They Crucified My Savior [but] He Rose." These events are reported in the Spirituals with an immediacy and poignancy which suggest intimate identification with the pain of human suffering and the joy of ultimate triumph.

So Incarnation receives only passing mention in the Spirituals. Passion and resurrection are more important themes. But the Spirituals most fully focus on those ways in which the living Christ interacts in the daily life of the slave, bringing counsel, comfort, and the hope of both temporal and eternal deliverance.

For instance, the intimacy between the believer and Christ is captured in the words from "Keep A-Inchin Along" which speak of ". . . you in the Lord and the Lord in you." Even though Jesus is "King Emanuel" who "rides on a milk-white horse," as other songs say, he is an approachable king. This king is a "brother" whose power is a resource rather than a threat, at least to the faithful. He is a personal friend with whom one can "meet and talk." Even in the most troubling and anxious life moments, "A Liitle Talk with Jesus Makes It Right."

Jesus' love is not divorced from justice: Jesus is "writing all the time," keeping account of one's deeds, and Christians are admonished to be mindful of how they live. But the clear sense conveyed in the Spirituals is that the justice of Jesus is not harsh; Jesus seeks to save rather than condemn. He is always knocking at the door of sinners, desiring to come in as savior. And Jesus is the refuge, the one who beckons his own to safety and security. Hence, now and at life's end, one may "Steal Away to Jesus."

Finally, Jesus is the effector of liberation. He breaks the bonds on the spirit, for as one song says,

"He came down here, and he talked to me,
Went away and left me free."

The Spirituals do not often speak directly of physical liberation from bondage. But there are clear indications that Jesus, as participant in the Godhead, could be depended upon to address this vital concern at some appointed time, for

"Didn't my Lord deliver Daniel?
An' why not everyman."

III. TWENTIETH-CENTURY DEVOTIONAL MATERIALS

When we move ahead in time to the twentieth century, we find that the songs, prayers, and other devotional elements employed by black Christians reflect a conception of Christ not unlike that found in the Spirituals.

Jesus is experienced as someone precious and beautiful. In countless sermons and prayers he has been referred to as the "Rose of Sharon," the "fairest of ten thousand," the "Lily of the Valley," the "pearl of great price." Such phrases point, of course, not to Jesus the physical form, but to the Christ as he has been encountered spiritually in one's life. It is not simply pietistic hyperbole when believers have sung "You can have all this world, but give me Jesus."

Jesus is the sustainer. He is said, in song and sermon, to be "water in dry places," "a rock in a weary land," "a shelter in the time of storm." One of the pieces of black devotional life best known in the larger world is Thomas Dorsey's song "Precious Lord." It captures much of black Christians' understanding of Christ as a living presence, available for support and guidance on life's difficult journey. One can ask confidently,

"When my way grows drear,
Precious Lord linger near. . .
Hear my cry, hear my call.
Hold my hand, lest I fall."

In a similar vein, Jesus is one's help when all others fail. He is "a lawyer who never lost a case," "a doctor who never lost a patient," "a way-maker—he can make a way out of no way."

And so, again, the Christological question is addressed not in metaphysical or ontological terms but rather from the standpoint of vital, personal pragmatics: Christ is what he does; he is what one experiences of him. It has always been granted that he is the Son of God, the divine Savior who redeems from sin. I recall an elderly deaconness in my congregation who, in prayer one Sunday morning, offered these words:

> I thank you (Jesus) for the blood you shedded over yonder on Calvary's hill. An' I thank you that a few drops spilled down through the corridors of time to cover my sins.

But the theological particulars of Sonship and atonement are not explored in the way the Church Councils or later church theologians have done. And while being converted and "saved" has important implications for a future life, the focus has been on the present: salvation has been seen as the inauguration of an intimate relationship with the Godhead in which Christ now assumes for one the roles I have discussed above—precious friend and sustainer, a source of security in an otherwise insecure existence.

One can detect in the Spirituals and in other black devotional literature a blurring of lines between Jesus the Christ and the God of the Hebrew Scriptures, as well as an indication of a pre-existent Son. For the persons of the Trinity are referred to interchangeably. I think this reflects not so much a confusion of function as it does black Christians' sense of the unity of function of the Trinitarian personae, who are experienced historically as three but, in fact, are one.

IV. TWENTIETH-CENTURY BLACK THEOLOGIANS

In the writings and pronouncements of black theologians in the present century, the Christological images of the Negro Spirituals and of early twentieth century devotional materials are extended into the image of Christ, the Liberator.

In a 1971 article entitled, "Black Consciousness in Theological Perspective," Dr. J. Deotis Roberts said that Jesus, as the Incarnation of God, demonstrates the love, justice, and mercy of God. As Jesus focuses our attention upon the will of God as revealed in the prophets and in his own life, said Roberts, we can discern the basis for a black theology which can assure that amidst all the oppression and abuse of life, the lovingly just and merciful God "is lord over life and lord of history and will have the last word."[5]

Similarly, Dr. James Cone, whose name has become synonymous with black theology, wrote in "The Sources and Norm of Black Theology" that Jesus is the complete revelation of God, showing us "who God is by what He does on behalf of the oppressed." Resurrection, said Cone, means Christ's continuing presence throughout the world for the purpose of liberating the oppresssed.[6] Cone addresses the subject again in his volume *God of the Oppressed*. Here he asserts that the crux of the Christological issue is the identity of Jesus in terms of our contemporary situation. For Cone, the connection point is that

> . . . the story of [Jesus'] life and death is the answer to the human story of oppression and suffering. . . . If our existence were not at stake . . . then the christological question would be no more than an intellectual exercise for professional theologians. But for Christians who have experienced the extreme absurdities of life, the christological question is not primarily theoretical but practical. It arises from the encounter of Christ in the struggle for freedom.[7]

And so for Cone, God's incarnation in Jesus, a *Jew,* identifies God in history with the oppressed. And in the crucifixion, God demonstrates God's willingness to suffer for the liberation of oppressed humanity. "The resurrection," says Cone, "is God's conquest of oppression and injustice. . . . It is the actualization in history of Jesus' eschatological vision that the last shall be first and the first last."[8]

Professor Jacqueline Grant, of the Interdenominational Theological Center, draws upon some of Cone's ideas in her "womanist theology." For her, Jesus is "the divine co-sufferer," who identifies with "the least of these." In America, this points to black women, with their tridimensional social disability as black, female, and poor. While affirming that Jesus is God incarnate, as according to church tradition, Grant understands the cross to image the conditions of black people today, and by extension all categories of the oppressed. And, says Grant,

> As the resurrection signified that there is more to life than the cross of Jesus

> Christ, for Black women it signifies that their tridimensional oppressive existence is not the end, but it merely represents the context in which a particular people struggle to experience hope and liberation.[9]

The late Rt. Rev. Joseph A. Johnson, bishop of the Christian Methodist Episcopal Church, wrote of "Jesus the Liberator." Johnson focused upon the "genuine humanity" of Jesus, even discounting the initiation of the Holy Spirit in Jesus' birth. For Bishop Johnson, a New Testament Ph.D., Christology was not a metaphysical inquiry into the nature of Christ. Rather, it was an attempt to understand God in the context of what God has wrought in the Christ event, with its soteriological and eschatological implications.[10]

Beyond these individual voices, and others that could be cited, several corporate statements have been issued bearing these same tones. For instance, the clergy and lay delegates to the 1976 General Conference of the African Methodist Episcopal Church adopted a "Black Position Paper" which declared that

> God's work of salvation in Jesus Christ is human liberation. . . . The Christological implications are implicit in the prophetic tradition. Jesus applies this tradition to himself [in Luke 4:18]. . . . It is God's will that all opressive forces be done away with. This is the meaning of the Exodus and the Incarnation. It is also the meaning of the Crucifixion and the Resurrection.[11]

In the same year, the National Conference of Black Churchmen published a statement authored by its Theological Commission that illuminates the posited connection between biblical and Christological themes, on the one hand, and the situation of the oppressed on the other. The Statement says that,

> Black Theology symbolizes Jesus Christ as the Black Messiah to remind Black people, in the most forceful manner, that God, through Christ, takes upon himself the badge of their suffering humiliation and struggle, transforming it by the triumph of his resurrection.

The Statement continues that blackness has been historically the signpost of undeserved suffering and oppression for persons of African descent. In Christ's resurrection, God achieved and proclaimed victory over the forces of oppression—not just for Jesus, but for every person, for every region, for all time. The statement asserts that black Christians identify the passion/resurrection story as a paradigm of their own situation. And, projecting blackness as a symbol for all human oppression, they see the Christ as the Black Messiah. God's victory in the Christ event is the hope and promise of all people suffering oppression, whether racial or gender or economic, religious, or physical capability, or whatever the type of the oppression.[12]

In 1977 the National Conference of the Black Theology Project (a body composed of clergy, laity, and academics), adopted a "Message to the Black Church and Community" which spoke of "Jesus Christ, the Black Messiah and Liberator." It asserted that, "In those places where pain was the deepest and suffering the most severe, there Jesus lived and suffered, died and was resurrected."[13]

V. THE SEED GROUND FOR INCARNATION/CHRISTOLOGY IMAGES

The religious background of Africans imported to this country as slaves provided fertile seed ground for the planting of Christianity. African traditional religion, in its multiple expressions across the continent, affirmed a supreme, creator God whose benevolent concern for earth and its people was shown in daily, intimate superintendence of the created order. Directly, and through lesser governing spirits, God ordered and sustained life. For humans, God was, in the words of one aphorism, "the one on whom men lean and do not fall." God expected humans to honor the virtues of kindness, supportive care for the animate as well as inanimate arenas of creation, respect for community, personal industry, and the like. The prohibitions that the Judeo-Christian tradition knows in its Ten Commandments were held to be binding. Amongst the various peoples of the African continent one could also find myths of creation, acts by primordials which precipitate divine-human physical separation (cf. the "fall"), a general flood, God's commissioning of certain individuals (in one case, God's son) to deliver a people, divine judgment, with reward and punishment. So the Christianity brought to slaves was not planted in totally foreign soil.

Some emphases, however, were different. African traditions focused on the present life; it was here that rewards and punishments generally were meted out. Sin was understood in terms of one's support of or violation of the integrity of life in community, rather than the violation of codified divine laws. A good life could lead to elevation to ancestorhood, or at least to fond retention in the collective memory of the community. But the afterlife was a fairly nondescript place. It was a future neither to be striven for nor to be much concerned about. So one lived toward a favored status in the community's past rather than in one's individual future.

This was the religious milieu of the imported African into which Christianity was introduced. Those African Americans who were convicted by the faith accepted its basic doctrinal tenets, such as a loving trinitarian creator, the Incarnation of God in Jesus, whose life and death redeems humanity from the consequences of its sinfulness, the unity of all Christians, a future life of reward and punishment. But the contexts of slavery and oppression have made for some particular emphases.

African Americans have appreciated the reality of sin and its consequences. For instance, in the Negro Spirituals there are appeals such as,

> Sinner please don't let this harvest pass
> And die and lose your soul at last.

or

> Mind out, my brother, how you walk on the cross;
> Your foot might slip and your soul be lost.

Noted nineteenth century black pastor Rev. Henry Highland Garnett admonished slaves to seek their freedom so that the slavery system could not coerce them to do wrong nor inhibit them from fulfilling Christian duty. Slavery, as such, said Garnett, would not excuse them from God's awful penalties for unfaithful living. And twentieth-century black Christians could be heard to sing,

> I once was lost in sin
> But Jesus took me in.

Yet, the sin which has been experienced by African Americans as the most fraught with existential anxiety and pervasive consequences has not been their own misdoings or unfaithfulness. It has been the sins visited upon them by others, proscribing their lives and assaulting their deep-most selves. From this sin they have most fervently sought redemption. Their reading of Scripture revealed a God who had acted in history to redeem God's people from human oppression and who could be depended upon so to act again. In the Old Testament, Moses was God's chief emissary of redemption. In the New Testament, God acted in a special way through Jesus. For black Christians, the embodiment of God in Jesus was a definitive identification with their own situation: humbly born under rude circumstances, rejected and ill-treated in his living, dying a violent, ignominious death. Says the old, popular song "Sweet Little Jesus Boy,"

> The world treat you mean, Lord;
> Treats me mean, too.

But God would have the last word. There is, perhaps, no sermonic phrase received as more thrilling in black congregations than "But on the third day morning. . . ." These words begin the affirmation that in resurrection Jesus the Christ achieved victory over the oppressive, death-dealing forces of the world. It became a widespread tradition in black homiletics for nearly every sermon to "stop by Calvary" and go on to Easter. For in bursting forth from the grave, the preacher would say, Jesus "placed one foot in time and one foot in eternity and proclaimed 'I am he that was dead but am alive forevermore'." For black Christians, pressed down under the weight of this world's rulers, how ultimately reassuring that in the passion/resurrection drama, "the kingdoms of this world [had] become the Kingdoms of our Lord and of His Christ."

No black triumphalism should be read in here. Black Christians have not typically claimed that blacks, *per se,* are special or prior objects of God's concern. As has been commonly heard in black Christian circles, "God is no respector of persons." Rather, God is understood to stand over against all structures of oppression, seeking to bring all persons into a reconciled community of love and justice.

Herein has been the focus of Incarnation and Christology for African Americans. God, through Christ, embodied their condition and conclusively demonstrated the power to effect their salvation, both temporal and eternal. They bear testimony to the working of that power in the unfolding of their individual and corporate lives. And so, when one seeks the Christological understanding of African American Christians over the years, one discovers images bearing a continuity from generation to generation. The images have honored the biblical witness and the theological traditions of the church as received. But they also reflect the peoples' experience of Christ, as shaped by the religious, social, and personal contexts in which the divine has been encountered. This, of course, is not different from the processes by which other individuals and groups have arrived at their Christological images. It only reveals one faithful particularization of the faith held by all those who have bound themselves to the "one Lord, one faith, one baptism."

NOTES

1. Quoted in Benjamin Mays, *The Negro's God* (New York: Atheneum, 1968) 42.

2. Cf. Robert Bennett, "Biblical Hermeneutics and the Black Preacher," *Journal of the Interdenominational Theological Center,* II Spring 1974. 38-53.

3. Cf. Richard Allen, *The Life Experience and Gospel Labors of the Rt. Rev. Richard Allen* (New York: Abingdon Press, 1960) 69-74.

4. James Weldon Johnson and J. Rosamond Johnson, *The Books of American Negro Spirituals.* Two volumes in one (New York: Viking Press, 1926) II, 14f. Most Spirituals cited in this paper may be found in this collection.

5. Reprinted in C. Eric Lincoln, ed., *The Black Experience in Religion* (Garden City, NY: Anchor Press, 1974) 99-109.

6. Ibid., 110-126.

7. James H. Cone, *God of the Oppressed* (New York: Seabury Press, 1975) 108-109.

8. Ibid., 135.

9. Cf. "Womanist Theology: Black Womens' Experience as a Source for Doing Theology, with Special Reference to Christology," in Gayraud S. Wilmore, ed., *African American Religious Studies: An Interdisciplinary Anthology* (Durham: Duke University Press, 1989) 208-227.

10. Ibid., 126-138.

11. The "Position Paper" is reprinted in Gayraud S. Wilmore and James H. Cone, *Black Theology: A Documentary History, 1966-1979* (Maryknoll, NY: Orbis Books, 1979) 288-95.

12. Ibid., 340-44.

13. Ibid., 345-49.

TRINITY AND INCARNATION: IN SEARCH OF CONTEMPORARY ORTHODOXY

COLIN BROWN

To many Christians the doctrine of the Trinity is perplexing, irrelevant, and best left alone. For practical purposes they solve the problem in one of two ways. One way is to follow in the footsteps of the nineteenth century father of liberal theology, Friedrich Schleiermacher, and postpone thinking about it for as long as possible. Schleiermacher did so on the grounds that the doctrine is "not an immediate testimony about Christian selfconsciousness, but only a collection of several such testimonies."[1] The other way of dealing with the Trinity is to practise tritheism in all but name. Thus the Father, the Son, and the Holy Spirit are worshipped as three separate deities and assigned separate functions. Such a practice stops short of fully fledged tritheism by making the proviso that the deities are all of the same divine substance, and are thus ultimately one. This is the route apparently favored by those who would solve the male gender problem of God by speaking of "Creator, Redeemer, and Sustainer" instead of "Father, Son, and Holy Spirit."

But among scholars the Trinity remains a vital issue, and many see it as the most basic and important of all doctrines.[2] A full-scale examination of the contemporary scene lies beyond the scope of this paper. My aim is restricted to three goals. First, I shall take note of three streams of thought. Second, I shall make some observations. Third, I shall offer some thoughts on what might be called the Trinitarian witness of the Gospels. The outcome will be (I hope) an indication of the lines on which an orthodox approach may be restated.

I. THREE STREAMS OF THOUGHT

A. The Monotheistic Tradition.

Doctrines of the Trinity fall into two main groups: those which stress the oneness of God and those which stress God's threeness. Although it is somewhat out of fashion at the moment, I shall start with the former and Karl Barth's landmark discussion.

Barth saw himself as something of an innovator and revisionist, though he stood firmly in the tradition of Jewish monotheism and its proclamation: "Hear, O Israel: The LORD our God is one LORD; and you shall love the LORD your God with all your heart, and with all your soul, and with all your might" (Deut 6: 4-5). Barth broke with custom by treating the Trinity at the beginning of his *Church Dogmatics* in his *Prolegomena*. In systematic theology prolegomena deal with things that have to be said first, like "How do we know?" and "What do we know?" Barth said that all this really comes under the heading of the Trinity. For the doctrine of the Trinity was nothing less than Barth's principle of knowledge. Only God can reveal God. The Father reveals himself in the Son through the power of the Spirit. Revelation is "the root of the Doctrine of the Trinity."[3] The doctrine of the Trinity was none other than the attempt to state what we know and how we know in the process of God's self-revelation in God's dealings with humankind.

Barth not only called for a revision of the role and place of the doctrine. He also called for semantic changes. To talk about the Trinity was not to talk about three centers of consciousness—or three divine I's—acting in concert. It was, rather, to talk about the *one divine I* three times over. Hence it was misleading and unhistorical to apply modern ideas of personality to the three members of the Trinity.[4] For *person* suggests an individual center of consciousness with mind, will, and emotions. Barth protested that such a view was not intended by the church fathers who originally coined the terminology, and it was far removed from the thought of such founders and shapers of Western theology as Augustine, Aquinas, and Calvin.

For Augustine, the human soul or mind with its memory, understanding, and will was a model for thinking about the Trinity.[5] As the image of God, it exhibited a unity in threefoldness. Memory, understanding and will were all functions of the mind in its totality. They were distinct but not separate. To Thomas Aquinas, the *persons* were "realities subsisting in the divine nature."[6] To Calvin, *person* meant "a 'subsistence' in God's essence."[7] Barth's proposal was an updated version of this kind of thinking. Although he was doubtful whether it would win widespread acceptance, Barth suggested the German term *Seinsweise* (literally "way of being" or "mode of being") as an alternative to *person*.[8] He did not see himself as a modalist in the conventional sense of treating the three modes of God's being as temporary manifestations or three ways of looking at God. Rather, the three *Seinsweisen* were three ways in which God was eternally God.

The Jesuit theologian, Karl Rahner, presents a Roman Catholic counterpart. Like Barth, he warns against the anachronistic misreading of the term *person* with the unfortunate implication that it means three distinct "personalities" in God. Rather, we must say that "the one God subsists in three distinct manners of subsisting . . . the Father, the Son, and Spirit are the one God each in a different manner of subsisting and in this sense we may count 'three' in God."[9] To Rahner, the mystery of the Trinity is grounded in the mystery of biblical monotheism. "Throughout the Old Testament there runs the basic theme that God is the absolute mystery, whom nobody can see without dying, and that it is nevertheless this God himself who conversed with the Fathers through his actions in history. This revealing self-manifestation is, in the Old Testament, mediated mostly . . . by the 'Word,' which, while causing God to be present in power, also represents him; and by the 'Spirit,' who helps men to understand and to announce the Word. When these two are not active, Yahweh has retreated from his people . . . . (The Torah and Wisdom doctrine of sapiential literature is only a more individualistic version of the same basic conception. It pays less attention to historical development.) God is present in the unity of Word and Spirit. "[10]

B. Social Trinitarianism

In marked contrast to Barth and Rahner with their stress on the oneness of God subsisting in three ways are those theologians who stress God's threeness. To them, the Trinity is a divine society. Moltmann speaks for many, when he shrugs aside the charges of Barth and Rahner that social Trinitarians have read back modern notions of personhood into the traditional terminology. He dismisses the charge of tritheism, and counterattacks Barth and Rahner for entertaining monolithic, monarchian, and even idealistic views of God. It is they who have defective views of personhood. "Without social relation there can be no personality."[11] One is reminded of the song "People who need people are the luckiest people in the world . . . . " Not even God can be a person without other persons.

This idea is not exactly new. It has been traced back to the speculative reasoning of Richard of St. Victor in the twelfth century.[12] To a modern social Trinitarian like Cornelius Plantinga, Jr., "the Holy Trinity is a divine, transcendent society or community of three fully personal and fully divine entities: the Father, the Son, and the Holy Spirit or Paraclete" who are "wonderfully unified by their common divinity."[13] Indeed, the term *God* is merely an abstraction for this "common divinity" or "divine essence" which only becomes *concrete* in the three persons.[14]

The social Trinitarians work out their positions in accordance with their particular agendas. To Moltmann, the cross reveals God as *a suffering God* who identifies himself with the suffering of the world. The suffering is *Trinitarian* in that the suffering that the Son experiences in his death is different from the suffering experienced by the Father through the suffering of his Son.[15] The theme of the crucified God is the center of all theology.[16] Other theologians are less ready to give up divine immutability and impassibility. Conscious of their vulnerability to charges of tritheism, social Trinitarians strive to show that the Father-Son-Spirit language of the New Testament not only points to God as a divine society, but is also logically coherent. To them, theology took a wrong turn with Augustine whose views were out of line with what they consider to be the main stream of patristic thought.

C. The Abandonment of Trinitarian Thinking

Alongside these two streams is a third stream which openly or tacitly abandons Trinitarian thinking altogether. An example of the latter is D.M. Baillie's influential book *God Was in Christ*.[17] Baillie insisted that the starting point for Christology today must be the fact that Jesus was a particular, historical human being. At the same time recognition must also be given to the fact that people down the ages have found God through him. But Baillie also believed that many traditional approaches to Christology lead to dead ends.

A case in point was the doctrine of *kenosis* or "emptying" which gets its name from the statement in Phil 2:6-7 which declares that Christ Jesus "though he was in the form of God, did not count equality with God a thing to be grasped, but emptied himself and took the form of a servant, being born in the likeness of men" (RSV). The doctrine was designed to show how the incarnation of the Second Person of the Trinity might be feasible.[18] By laying aside or not using such divine attributes as omnipotence, omniscience, and omnipresence, Christ could be fully divine yet exist in human form. Plausible as this might seem, it raised for Baillie and others more problems than it solved. What became of the cosmic functions of the Second Person of the Trinity during the earthly period in which they were laid aside? But the alternative was equally implausible. Was it feasible to think of the human body of the infant Jesus asleep in the manger as the control center of the universe from which the divine Logos sustained and ordered all things?

Baillie's answer was to sidestep such problems by taking the paradox of grace as a model for approaching the question of the Incamation. In grace the believer experiences the power and love of God while still remaining human in every sense of the term. Could not Jesus be the supreme example of the grace of the Father active in a human life?[19] Was not this the point of the apostle Paul's great affirmation that "God was in Christ reconciling the world to himself" (2 Cor 5: 18) from which Baillie got the title for his book? Jesus repeatedly pointed people away from himself to the Father. According to the Fourth Gospel, he attributed his works not to himself but to the Father. "Do you not believe that I am in the Father and the Father in me? The words that I say to you I do not speak on my own authority; but the Father who dwells in me does his works" (John 14: 10).

What are we to make of Baillie's reconstruction? In the end I am left with the impression that for Baillie the Incarnation is *an Incarnation of the Father* in the mold of Schleiermacher. To Schleiermacher, Jesus was "like all other human beings in virtue of the sameness of human nature, but different from all others through the constant potency of his awareness of God, which was an actual existence of God in him."[20]

Whereas Baillie seems to teach the incarnation of the Father, advocates of *Spirit Christology* seem to prefer an incarnation of the Spirit by presenting the "divinity" of Christ in terms of the activity of the Spirit in this life. G.W.H. Lampe advocated an "inspirational" Christology as opposed to the "incarnational" theology of orthodoxy. But in any case Lampe made it clear that when he spoke of the Spirit, he was not thinking of the Third Person of the Trinity but was merely employing a figure of speech for the immanent creativity of God.[21] James D.G. Dunn agrees that in pre-Christian Judaism there is nothing to suggest the Spirit as a *hypostasis* or "entity in any sense independent of God" and no thought of an incarnation of the Spirit.[22] Dunn thinks that Jesus himself "*seems to have understood the relationship between himself and the Spirit in terms primarily of inspiration and empowering*, that is, as the power of God himself filling him and coming to manifestation through him."[23] The first Christians, perhaps including Paul, likewise understood the relation between the earthly Jesus and the Spirit in terms of inspiration and empowering. At any rate Dunn sees no place in early New Testament Christianity for the idea of incarnation in the sense of a pre-existent divine person (in the social Trinitarian sense) entering into the human body of Jesus who would thus combine in himself a human person and a divine person.

II. SOME OBSERVATIONS

A. The Danger of Specialization

Although the Trinity is much debated, there often seems to be an unfortunate division of labor among scholars. Perhaps this is due to the intense pressure to specialize. The result is that some books are written by philosophers, while others are written by biblical scholars, historians, or theologians. This leads to the further result that a book on the Trinity written by a philosopher might display dazzling virtuosity in logical analysis or metaphysical speculation. But if it is all based on a naive view of the term "person" and lack of understanding biblical language, the end product is apt to be something like what Anselm had in mind when he spoke of beautiful pictures painted on water or in air.[24] The same can, of course, apply to the pronouncements of theologians or biblical scholars who forge ahead with scant regard to philosophy or history. Guessing is always hazardous, but if I were to hazard a guess about the state of play in the contemporary discussion, I would say something like this. The majority of philosophers and systematic theologians seem to favor some form of social Trinitarianism, whereas the mood among biblical scholars supports some form of monotheism which questions the propriety of reading our conceptual schemes back into Scripture.

B. The Concept of Person

A case in point is the repeated assertion of the social Trinitarians that in order to be a person one needs other persons. Therefore, it makes sense to think of God as a society of persons. There is certainly something powerful and appealing about this idea. But once one starts down this road it is difficult to stop. For in order to be a truly human person one needs more than a society of two others. Indeed, one needs relations with the opposite sex. The man needs mother, grandmother, sister, wife, daughter, granddaughter, aunt, friend, in order to enter into the full range of personal relationships. Women are persons *as women*; men are persons *as men*. Are we not pointed beyond the all-male trio of social Trinitarianism to the gods and goddesses of polytheism as the symbolic counterpart to our personhood and the transcendent cause of our universe?

One can think of several possible replies to this question. The first is simply to accept its logic and abandon Trinitarianism altogether. Clearly such a response would be unacceptable to the social Trinitarians. A second answer might break with the main stream of tradition and identify the Holy Spirit as the divine mother, though few so far have followed this path to the end.[25] A third answer might reply that sexuality is a mark of creatureliness rather than personhood, and thus we need not apply it to God. But if sexuality—not simply sexual activity—which is so deeply ingrained into our personhood is not an essential characteristic of divine personhood, one is left wondering whether the social Trinitarian understanding of relational personhood is equally inapplicable to God. The problem becomes even more acute if one wants to deny sexuality to God, while retaining the language of begetting. However, this whole line of thinking looks increasingly like a piece of hypothetical rationalization invoked to justify the term person when applied to God in the social Trinitarian sense. A fourth possible reply is simply to say that as a sheer matter of fact the Christian tradition is rooted in the testimony of Scripture to God as Father, Son, and Holy Spirit. And with this we are brought back to the central question. What do we mean when we use this language?

C. Son-of-God Language

The crux of the matter lies in how we understand the term "Son of God" and the questions that it poses about the relation of Jesus to the one whom he called Father and to the Spirit that came upon him after his baptism. The point is illustrated by the cheerful retort of Cornelius Plantinga to the charge that social Trinitarians are really tritheists: "If it is tritheist to believe that *Father, Son,* and *Spirit* designate distinct persons, then Paul and the author of the Fourth Gospel must be regarded as tritheists. And they are good company to keep."[26] But to say this is to beg the question. For the claim simply asserts what has not been demonstrated. Indeed, it seems to entail a systematic misunderstanding of Son-of-God language in Scripture.

James D.G. Dunn speaks for many biblical scholars when he concludes that, "*The NT contains a diversity of christologies of Jesus' divine sonship and to merge them into one common theme is to run the risk of denying the distinctive emphases of each.*"[27] Indeed, one may well ask whether the term "Son of God" is in and of itself a divine title at all. Certainly there are many instances in biblical language where it is definitely not a designation of deity. Adam is called "the son of God" in Luke's genealogy of Jesus (Luke 3: 38). Hosea 11:1 (which is cited in Matt 2: 15) alludes to the nation of Israel as God's son. In Wisdom 2: 18 the righteous man is called God's son. Nathan's prophecy to David contains God's promise to David's successor: "I will be his father, and he shall be my son" (2 Sam 7:14; cf. Psalm 89: 26-27). This passage also occurs in a collection of testimonies at Qumran (4QFlor 10f.), indicating that the messianic significance of this prophecy was a matter of continuing speculation in first century Judaism. In Psalm 2: 7 the anointed king is addressed at his installation: "You are my son, today I have begotten you" (cited in Acts 13: 33; Heb. 1: 5; 5: 5; cf. 2 Pet 1: 17). This passage is the source of the identification of Jesus with God's Son by the *Bat Qol* (voice from heaven) after his baptism (Mark 1: 11; Matt 3: 17; Luke 3: 22; cf. John 1: 34). The voice also identifies Jesus with the chosen servant in whom God delights (Isa. 42: 1; cf. also Matt 12: 18-21).

In the light of these passages in their context, the title " Son of God" is not in itself a designation of personal deity or an expression of metaphysical distinctions within the Godhead. Indeed, to be a "Son of God" one has to be a being who is *not* God! It is a designation for a creature indicating a special relationship with God. In particular, it denotes God's representative, God's vice-regent. It is a designation of kingship, identifying the king as God's son.[28] Therefore, I take the application of the title "Son of God" at his baptism to be an affirmation of Jesus as God's Son-king in virtue of his anointing by the Spirit. Likewise C.F.D. Moule comments on the trial scene: "In Mark 14: 61 the High Priest's words, 'Are you the Christ, the son of the Blessed One?' are presumably understood by the Evangelist as a question about a Messianic claim"[29] The title expresses the intimate relationship which Jesus had through the Spirit with the Father as the Father's anointed representative, which is depicted in the Gospel narratives culminating in his death and the cry of dereliction, "My God, my God, why have you forsaken me?" (Matt 27: 46; Mark 15: 34).

I believe that this is the meaning that we should attach to the term "Son of God" at the beginning of Mark's Gospel (Mark 1: 1) in view of the account of the baptism, anointing and voice from heaven which quickly follows. Nor can we read the theology of later centuries into the testimony of the centurion at the foot of the cross: "Truly this man was a son of God" (Mark 15: 39; Matt 27: 54; cf. Luke 23: 47 "Certainly this man was innocent!"). In my view the term "Son of God" ultimately converges on the term "image of God," which is to be understood as God's representative, the one in whom God's Spirit dwells, and who is given stewardship and authority to act on God's behalf.[30] The designation of Jesus as "Son of God in power according to the Spirit of holiness by his resurrection from the dead" (Rom 1: 4) is a reaffirmation of that Son-kingship with divine authority, insofar as by the resurrection the Spirit has overturned the negative verdict of the

Sanhedrin in condemning Jesus to death as a blasphemer who sought to lead Israel astray.[31]

Let me pause here to stress what exactly I am trying to do. A social Trinitarian might wonder if this line of thought tends to diminish the personal divinity of Christ. My point is exactly the opposite. I am trying to understand how the New Testament presents Jesus as the Christ,[32] and on that basis construct our understanding of Jesus' divinity and of the Trinity. It is not the title "Son of God" which defines Jesus; it is Jesus who redefines the title in view of who he was and what he did.

It seems to me to be a fundamental mistake to treat statements in the Fourth Gospel about the Son and his relationship with the Father as expressions of inner-Trinitarian relationships. But this kind of systematic misreading of the Fourth Gospel seems to underlie much of social Trinitarian thinking. Thus statements like "I and the Father are one" (John 10: 30) and those about the mutual indwelling of Jesus and the Father (John 10: 38; 14: 10-11, 20; 17: 21, 23) are taken to be statements about inner relations of the "persons" of the Trinity.[33] However, the Fourth Gospel itself does not require such a reading.[34] When read in context, the statements are evidently statements about *Jesus' relationship with the Father on earth*.[35]

It is a common but patent misreading of the opening of John's Gospel to read it as if it said: "In the beginning was the *Son*, and the *Son* was with God, and the *Son* was God" (John 1: 1).[36] What has happened here is the substitution of *Son* for *Word* (Greek *logos*), and thereby the *Son* is made a member of the Godhead which existed from the beginning. But if we follow carefully the thought of John's Prologue, it is the *Word* that preexisted eternally with God and is God. The same Word that made all things and is the light that enlightens humankind "became flesh and dwelt among us, full of grace and truth; we have beheld his glory, glory as of the only Son from the Father" (John 1: 14; cf. vv. 3 and 8). In other words, Son-language in John denotes *the Word made flesh in Jesus* who as such speaks God's Word to human beings on earth.

Hippolytus of Rome put his finger on the key issue when he observed that "the Word was not a perfect Son when he was fleshless and on his own, although because he was Word, he was perfect Only-begotten. Nor could the flesh exist on its own apart from the Word, because it has its subsistence in the Word. So in this way a single perfect Son of God was made manifest."[37] But even this clear statement of the distinction between Word and Son contains the seeds of what was to become a source of endless problems in thinking about the Trinity. I refer to the description of the Word as "Only-begotten." Whereas the Fourth Gospel simply says that the Word was with God and was God in the beginning, the fathers of the second and third centuries began to talk about the *generation* of the Word.

Maurice Wiles has persuasively argued that the idea of "eternal generation" was bound up with the way that the early fathers interpreted the begetting of wisdom in Proverbs 8: 25 ("before the hills he begat me") and Psalm 110: 3 LXX ("before the morning star I begat thee").[38] However, the impetus for applying the thought of *begetting* to the generation of the second "person" of the Trinity would seem to be bound up with the designations "Son," "Father," and "person." If the first "person" is thought of as "Father," and the second as "Son" the question of their relationship is inevitable. Thus we have, in fact, *two acts of begetting*: one in time when Jesus was (in the language of the creeds) "conceived by the Holy Spirit," and one in eternity when (in the language of Origen) the unbegotten Father begat the Son "by an eternal act."[39]

Inevitably this latter formulation raises the question of whether there was a time when the Son did not exist. Origen sought to answer it with an analogy drawn from nature. The Son's generation is eternal and everlasting in a way comparable to the brilliancy of the sun and the sun itself. However, there was a price to be paid for such a maneuver, viz. that "eternal generation" is no longer understood as the personal activity of an individual possessing self-consciousness bringing into being another similar individual. It is, rather, a way of thinking about different aspects of the sun in which the burning of sun is perceived as light. The point was not lost on the modalists who used the same example for their own ends.[40]

One is left wondering whether the thorny questions of later ages might have been avoided if the church fathers had not embarked on the language of the "eternal generation" of the Son. How things might have been different, if the fathers had kept strictly to the language of John's Prologue as their paradigm for speaking of Trinity and Incarnation. What pre-exists is not the Son *per se,* but the Logos. In John the Logos is not begotten or generated. The Logos was with God and was God, and in the course of time became flesh as the Son.

D. *Kenosis,* a Problem Generated by Social Trinitarianism

Let me now return to the question of *kenosis,* and make the observation that *kenosis* is bound up with a social Trinitarian view of the Trinity and Incarnation. Some form of the doctrine of *kenosis* is inescapable, if we think of the Trinity as three separate persons or centers of divine consciousness and the Incarnation as what happens, when one of those *persons* becomes a human being. Something has got to give. The divine attributes have got to be laid aside, and the cosmic functions of that person have to be taken over for the time being by the other two.

In discussing D.M. Baillie we noted some of the consequent conundrums, but by no means exhausted the list. If Jesus' knowledge was limited and not basically different from the general state of knowledge of his time, could it be that Jesus was wrong on various matters? Could such limitations also extend to his moral character? But can we treat divine attributes like optional extras which an entity may or may not have and still remain the same essential entity? The situation is not like comparing two models of a car in a showroom, where the cheaper version is the basic model and the more expensive one is "loaded" with air conditioning, tinted glass, power steering, air bag, custom paint, etc. The divine attributes are not like the optional extras which make the "loaded" car more expensive. They are what makes God *God*. Without them God would not be *God*.

However, *kenosis* is not a problem for those who work with a different model of the Trinity. For the question of how God could be in Christ becomes a question of how might we think of divine immanence in human life. D.M. Baillie approached it by proposing the paradox of grace as a model for thinking how God could be present in human life without destroying our full humanity. Calvin approached it by asserting what came to be known as the *extra Calvinisticum*: "For even if the Word in his immeasurable essence united with the nature of man into one person, we do not imagine that he was confined therein. . . the Son of God descended from heaven in such a way that, without leaving heaven, he willed to be borne in the virgin's womb, to go about the earth, to hang upon the cross; yet he continuously filled the world even as he had done from the beginning."[41]

Perhaps Justin Martyr's explanation may also help. Justin distinguished between the eternal word immanent in God (*logos endiathetos*) and the exterior, temporal word put forth when God spoke (*logos prophorikos*). He argued that the divine word or reason was disseminated in the world generally, but was also expressed particularly in the Incarnation.[42] Justin observed that, when one expresses one's mind, the thoughts remain one's thoughts while at the same time they are expressed outside of oneself.[43] Likewise, God's Logos remains with God while being disseminated in the world in general and in Christ in particular.

My own proposal is an updated version of Justin and Calvin. If we think of a major international airport like LAX in Los Angeles, O'Hare in Chicago, or London's Heathrow, the planes on the ground and in the air come under the direction of the control tower. The mind and authority of the control tower is located in the control tower, but is expressed throughout the radius of its operation. It remains present, active, and authoritative within that radius. But it also may be present in a fuller way, if circumstances call for it and the controller relates to a particular plane in a particular way, and the pilot of that plane seeks more complete guidance and direction.

A model like this may help us better understand the intimacy which Jesus enjoyed with his Father whom he addressed with the familiar term *Abba* (Mark 14: 36).[44] Like the pilot in our illustration, he did not lose his human individuality. For guidance Jesus lived by God's word (e.g. Matt 4: 4; 5: 17), and turned in prayer to God as his Father, as he sought to discern his Father's will and further his kingdom (Matt 6: 9-13; Luke 11: 2-4).

Thus, we need not think of the human Jesus as the center of operations, a human walking control tower from which the operations of the entire universe were consciously or unconsciously controlled for a period of roughly thirty years. Nor do we have to think that the cosmic functions of the divine Logos were held in cold storage for a time or handed over to one or other members of the Trinity, until he could resume them. We certainly have to reckon with the divine condescension in which God comes to us, not in almighty power, but in love and on our creaturely level. But this is *a question of divine immanence*, and not the pseudo-problem of what happens if a divine being is encapsulated in a human container. In the language of the Fourth Gospel, the story of Jesus is the story of what happened, when the light that lightens everyone came into the world in the person of Jesus (John 1: 9). It is the story of what happened when the pre-existent Logos of God became flesh (John 1: 14).

But does not the Christ-hymn in Phil 2: 6-11 seem to demand some form of *kenosis* with its call to have the mind of Christ "who, though he was in the form of God did not count equality with God a thing to be grasped, but emptied himself, taking the form of a servant, being born in the likeness of men" (vv. 6-7)? In response I have to say that I agree with those scholars who say that the point of the hymn is not a comparison between Christ's pre-existent state as the divine Son in glory and his state of humiliation as a servant.[45] Rather, it is a comparison between Christ and Adam in which the term "form of God" is the equivalent of saying "image of God." Whereas Adam who was made to be God's image refused to be content with that and sought to be "like God" (Gen 2: 5), Jesus as God's Christ, the anointed messianic Son, chose the role of a servant. I would go further and say that there is a double focus here; there is also an echo of the temptation stories, where Jesus as the newly designated "Son of God" is tempted to use divine power for his own ends (Matt 4: 3-11; Luke 4: 3-13). In short, the emptying of Phil 2: 6 does not seem to me to have anything to do with a supposed metaphysical change of states, but has everything to do with the life of servanthood which Paul calls upon his readers to practise in following the servant Paul (Phil 1: 1; 3: 17) and, above all, Christ Jesus, the servant *par excellence* whose self-emptying culminated in the outpouring of his life on the cross (cf. Isa 53: 12).

E. A Theological Pilgrimage

Before I attempt to sketch my own approach, I would like to say something about my theological pilgrimage. For over thirty years Christology has been a central concern, beginning with my work on Karl Barth and extending through my doctoral research into what may roughly be called the first hundred years of the quest of the historical Jesus and the sundry other studies which followed this work.[46] Up to the mid-seventies I might have said that Barth's and Rahner's stress on the oneness of God and that of the social Trinitarians represented complementary approaches. Now I must confess that social Trinitarianism seems to border on the realm of myth, as defined by Earl R. MacCormac, i.e. "the false attribution of reality to a suggestive metaphor."[47]

In the light of the considerations noted above, it seems to me that a complex structure has been erected upon the systematic misunderstanding of biblical language of sonship. What seems to have happened with a number of issues that we have been considering—various ways of understanding *person*- and *Son*-language, "eternal generation," *kenosis*, and indeed the social Trinitarian approach—is the evolution of a series of interrelated protective lines of defence designed to safeguard central beliefs about God and Christ. In the course of time these protective lines have come to be felt to be a necessary part of orthodoxy. Although justification was sought for them in biblical language, they moved progressively away from the testimony of Scripture.

What turned my thoughts in a different direction and led me to develop an alternative approach to the Incarnation and Trinity was an invitation to write a book in the *I Believe* series on the subject of the miracles of Jesus. If I had written the book in the mid-seventies when the invitation came, I might have followed conventional lines arguing that, of course, Jesus could do miracles if he was the divine Son of God. Miracles were proof of his personal divinity. For various reasons the writing of the book got delayed. When at last I began research, the book took on a very different form and character. The outcome was *Miracles and the Critical Mind* (1984) and its less technical sequel *That You May Believe: Miracles and Faith, Then and Now* (1985).[48] Now I see the miracles not as the work of one member of the Trinity acting on his own, but like all God's works as ultimately the work of all three. In my concluding remarks I shall try to indicate how my research here has led me to a statement of orthodoxy which is genuinely Trinitarian (in the sense of Barth and Rahner) and which is thoroughly in line with the definition of the Council of Chalcedon (451) in its claim that Jesus the Christ was "consubstantial with the Father as regards his divinity, and the same consubstantial with us as regards his humanity; like us in all respects except for sin."

Before I do so I need to make one further comment about methodology. It has to do with the venerable strategy of approaching Christology from the standpoint of soteriology. This strategy which is linked with such illustrious names as Athanasius, Anselm, and Luther scarcely needs documentation. It seeks to show that Jesus the Savior must possess certain qualities in order to be our Savior: he must be human (though not a sinner) in order to be our representative, and divine in order to have enough power to do the job and in order to ensure that we will belong to God as a result of his action.

I see two major flaws in this approach. The first lies in the fact that this is a game which anyone can play and win, because one loads the dice so that it rolls the way one wants. Or, to put it another way, one puts into the equation what one wants to get out of it. It is a game which can be played by both the orthodox and the heterodox. The way Athanasius played it led to a vindication of Nicene orthodoxy. The way his Arian opponents played it led to different conclusions. They argued that Christ could not be consubstantial with the Father, because the Father is impassible, whereas Jesus as savior clearly suffered and died. One could say that Christ was *like God*, but he was not "the only true God" (John 17: 3).[49] Likewise kenotic christology protests that it wants to safeguard the full divinity of Christ, but it ends up with *something like divinity*, because it is a divinity shorn of divine attributes.

The second flaw is bound up with the difficulty of matching up the supposed divine logic of the Incarnation and Atonement with the events as they played themselves out here on earth. There often seems to be a credibility gap between what is put forward as the divine inner logic and the historical circumstances and motivation of personalities and events. My approach, therefore, is based on an attempt to understand the testimony contained in the Scriptures and reflect on its significance.

III. THE TRINITARIAN TESTIMONY OF THE GOSPELS

A. Early Christian Apologetics

I would like to start by noting a couple of passages in the Acts of the Apostles which seem at first sight very unpromising, because they appear to say so much less than we want them to say. The first is taken from the account of Peter's preaching at Pentecost: "Men of Israel, hear these words: Jesus of Nazareth, a man attested to you by God with mighty works and wonders and signs which God did through him in your midst, as you yourselves know " (Acts 2: 22). The second is drawn from Peter's proclamation to Cornelius and the first Gentile converts: "You know the word which he sent to Israel, preaching good news by Jesus Christ (he is Lord of all), the word which was proclaimed throughout all Judea, beginning from Galilee after the baptism which John preached: how God anointed Jesus of Nazareth with the Holy Spirit and power; how he went about doing good and healing all that were oppressed by the devil, for God was with him" (Acts 10: 36-38). In neither declaration is it said that Jesus did things because of his personal divinity. In the first passage Jesus is described as *a man attested by God*; his works are actually the *works which God did through him*. In the second passage his works are more specifically attributed to *God's anointing him with the Holy Spirit and power*; his actions in doing good and healing all that were oppressed by the devil show that God was with him.

These statements seem to downplay the notion of personal divinity. What, in fact, they do is to lay the foundations of what might be called a Trinitarian approach to Christology. I believe that these statements belong to the apologetic of early Christianity and its defence against the charges of the Jewish leadership that Jesus was really an evil doer, a blasphemer, a man possessed by Satan, who sought to lead Israel astray by his teaching and signs and wonders. They sum up the underlying strategy of the first three, if not all four Gospels, in their presentation of Jesus and their vindication of him against hostile charges.

B. The First Three Gospels.

Broadly speaking, Matthew, Mark, and Luke present *a Spirit Christology* accompanied by an *underlying word Christology.* All three highlight the baptism of Jesus, the consequent descent of the Spirit upon him, and the identification of him as God's Son (Mark 1: 9-11; Matt 3: 13-17; Luke 3: 21-22). In the light of what we said above about the meaning of the term "Son of God," Jesus has now been installed with authority as God's anointed Son-king, his vice-regent. The anointing by the Spirit is not some kind of extra boost to enable him to function better. It is the act which makes him the Messiah, the Christ, the anointed one. It is constitutive for his identity as the messianic Son. Prior to this event, he was the Messiah designate; the anointing makes him the anointed one, the Messiah.[50] The Gospels of Matthew and Luke forestall the question of adoptionism with their accounts of the role of the Spirit in the conception of Jesus (Matt 1: 18, 20; Luke 1: 35). Jesus was who he was because of the role of the Spirit from the first. But he did not enter into his messianic office until his anointing by the Spirit.

In the temptation stories which follow, the Spirit drives Jesus into the wilderness, where he is tempted (Mark 1: 12-13). In the accounts given by Matthew (4: 1-11) and Luke (4: 1-13), the temptations turn on Jesus' identity as the Son of God. The point of the temptations are not "If you are the Second Person of the Trinity . . . . " Rather, they turn on the identification of Jesus as the newly anointed messianic Son. If Jesus has got this power and authority, why not use it to further his purposes?

In Luke's account, on returning to Galilee "in the power of the Spirit" (Luke 4: 16) Jesus enters the synagogue at Capernaum, where he reads from the scroll of the prophet Isaiah: "The Spirit of the Lord is upon me, because he has anointed me to preach good news to the poor. He has sent me to proclaim release to the captives and recovering of sight to the blind, to set at liberty those who are oppressed, to proclaim the acceptable year of the Lord" (Luke 1: 18-19; citing Isa 61: 1-12). It is the anointing and empowering by the Spirit which define Jesus and mission. In Matthew Jesus' identity and mission is defined by a different passage from Isaiah which links Jesus with God's servant upon whom he will put his Spirit and who will reach out to the Gentiles. His actions are seen as the fulfillment of the prophecy, "Behold, my servant whom I have chosen, my beloved with whom my soul is well pleased. I will put my Spirit upon him, and he shall proclaim justice to the Gentiles . . . and in him will the Gentiles hope" (Matt 12: 17-21; citing Isa 42: 1-4). The fact that Jesus cast out demons by the Spirit indicates that "the kingdom of God has come upon you" (Matt 12: 28; cf. Luke 11: 20). Peter's confession of Jesus as "the Christ, the Son of the living God" (Matt 16: 17), "the Christ" (Mark 8: 29), "The Christ of God" (Luke 9: 20) are confessions that indeed Jesus is the one anointed by the Spirit and who, as such, is the messianic Son.

The attribution of Jesus' power and authority to the Spirit is a theme which stands out clearly in the Gospels, but it has been widely neglected in traditional theology, apologetics, and piety alike. I believe that the reason for the neglect is a desire to express the Incarnation in terms of a metaphysical divine sonship instead of allowing our ideas to be formed by the witness of the Gospels. This emphasis has led to an unfortunate neglect of the *Spirit Christology* which is fundamental to understanding the message of Matthew,

Mark, and Luke. But these evangelists also develop a concurrent Word or Wisdom Christology. Jesus proclaims the Gospel of God. He speaks with authority in calling the disciples and expelling the unclean spirits. The people are amazed at his "new teaching" and "authority." By Jesus' word the leper is made clean, and the paralytic is assured that his sins are forgiven. Jesus' sundry pronouncements concerning fellowship with sinners, fasting, new wine, and the sabbath are spoken with an authority above that of the scribes. He is the sower who sows the word of God. He not only lives by the word of God, he embodies the word of God. He is the divinely authorized and empowered agent through whom the Father speaks and is present (Matt 10: 40; 11: 27; Luke 10: 16, 22).[51] In Matthew and Luke Jesus is not only presented as a teacher of wisdom, he is the personal manifestion of God's wisdom in action.[52]

III. THE FOURTH GOSPEL

If Matthew, Mark, and Luke have an explicit Spirit Christology accompanied by an implicit Word Christology, John presents *an explicit Word Christology* accompanied by *an implicit Wisdom and Spirit Christology*. We have already noticed John's stress on the Word made flesh, thus becoming God's Son who uniquely reveals his glory and makes the Father known (John 1: 1-18). As the Word, he existed before all things; through Jesus the Father speaks his word. He is the Father's executor in all things (John 1: 3, 9; 3: 16-21, 31-36; 6: 33, 50, 58, 63; 7: 28; 8: 14-20; 10: 36; 16: 28; 17: 1-5, 17, 21-24). Such activities are in fact assigned to wisdom in the biblical wisdom literature tradition.[53] Jesus is the human embodiment of God's wisdom and its glory. The response to Jesus is the same as the way men respond to wisdom in wisdom literature. Alongside John's stress on the Word, there is a developing Spirit Christology. "He on whom you see the Spirit descend and remain, this is he who baptizes with the Holy Spirit" (John 1: 33). Unless one is born of water and the Spirit one cannot see the kingdom of God (John 3: 5). True worshippers must worship in Spirit and in truth (John 4: 23).

The paraclete sayings of John 14: 16-17, 25; 15: 26 and 16: 7-15 form a bridge between Jesus' possession of the Spirit and his bestowal of the Spirit. Like wisdom, the Spirit enlightens those who follow and leads them into truth and life. The world cannot receive the Spirit, but the disciples are reminded that the Spirit is already present: "You know him for he dwells with you, and will be in you" (John 14: 17). However, the Spirit is not given as an inner spring of living water until Jesus is glorified (John 7: 39). Finally, the risen Christ breathes on the disciples and says: "Receive the Holy Spirit" (John 20: 22). I see this as a kind of prophetic act in which the action illustrates and embodies the prophecy. It also recalls the LORD God breathing into man the breath of life (Gen. 2: 15; cf. Wis 15: 11, 15). The Greek word for Spirit is *pneuma*, meaning wind, moving air, or breath. Obviously it is this last sense that is present here. The divine breath which gave life to Jesus and made the word of the Father present in him is now bestowed upon the disciples to carry on his mission.

Whereas the first three Gospels stress the activity of the Spirit, the Fourth Gospel focuses on Jesus as the one who does the works of the Father (John 10: 37-38). He who has seen Jesus has seen the Father (John 14: 9). For it is the Father who dwells in Jesus who does his works (John 14: 10). One may be inclined to look at the Gospel material and ask "Who is doing what?" The Gospels answer this question by presenting the root of the doctrine of the Trinity and the Incarnation. The picture that they give is not of three divine beings with separate functions like creating, redeeming, and sustaining. It is one God who manifests himself as the Father, speaking his word or wisdom, through his life-giving breath. Just as we cannot speak without breath, the divine word of the Father is not uttered without the Father's divine breath. We are not speaking of three beings. Neither are we merely talking about "inspiration" in the sense of enlightenment. We are talking about the threefold God in human life, the God who always exists and acts in his threefoldness. As God draws near in this mystery of revelation, we are confonted with the mystery of the Trinity and Incarnation.

NOTES

1. *Der christliche Glaube,* (2nd ed. 1831) ed. Martin Redeker (Berlin: de Gruyter, 1960), 2: 458, #170 (author's translation).

2. Books on the Trinity since 1980 include Jürgen Moltmann, *The Trinity and the Kingdom* (San Francisco: Harper & Row, 1981); Robert W. Jenson, *The Triune Identity* (Philadelphia: Fortress Press, 1982); William J. Hill, *The Three Personed God: The Trinity as a Mystery of Salvation* (Washington, D.C.: Catholic University of America Press, 1982); Bertrand de Margerie, *The Christian Trinity in History,* Studies in Historical Theology 1 (Still River, MA: St. Bede's Publications, 1982); David Brown, *The Divine Trinity* (La Salle: Open Court, 1985); Edmund Hill, *The Mystery of the Trinity* (London: Chapman, 1985); Michael O'Carroll, *Trinitas: A Theological Encyclopedia of the Holy Trinity* (Wilmington: Michael Glazier, 1987); Leonardo Boff, *Trinity and Society* (Maryknoll, NY: Orbis Books, 1988); R.P.C. Hanson, *The Search for the Christian Doctrine of God: The Arian Controversy 318-381* (Edinburgh: T. & T. Clark, 1988); Thomas F. Torrance, *The Trinitarian Faith: The Evangelical Theology of the Ancient Catholic Church* (Edinburgh: T. & T. Clark, 1988); Ronald J. Feenstra and Cornelius Plantinga, Jr., eds., *Trinity, Incarnation, and Atonement: Philosophical and Theological Essays* (Notre Dame: University of Notre Dame Press, 1989); John J. O'Donnell, *The Mystery of the Triune God* (New York/Mahwah: Paulist Press, 1989); Colin E. Gunton, *The Promise of Trinitarian Theology* (Edinburgh: T. & T. Clark, 1991).

Earlier works include Karl Barth, *Church Dogmatics* (Edinburgh: T. & T. Clark, 1,1 [1936] new translation, 1975, 1,2, 1956); Leonard Hodgson, *The Doctrine of the Trinity* (Digswell Place: Nisbet, 1943); Edmund J. Fortman, *The Triune God: A Historical Study of the Doctrine of the Trinity* (Philadelphia: Westminster Press; London: Hutchinson, 1972); Karl Rahner, *The Trinity* (New York: Seabury Press, 1974).

3. *Church Dogmatics* 1,1, 304-333

4. Ibid., 1,1, 353-368.

5. *On the Trinity* 10, 11,

6. *Summa Theologica* 1 ,30,1.

7. *Institutes* 1,13,6, Library of Christian Classics 20 (Philadelphia: Westminster Press, 1960) 128.

8. *Church Dogmatics* 1,1, 358-361.

9. *The Trinity,* 113-114.

10. Ibid., 41.

11. *The Trinity and the Kingdom,* 145.

12. Gunton, *The Promise of Trinitarian Theology,* 91-92; cf. Richard of St. Victor, *De Trinitate* 3, 19.

13. Feenstra and Plantinga, eds., *Trinity, Incarnation, and Atonement,* 27. Plantinga has also written the article on "Trinity" in *The International Standard Bible Encyclopedia* 4 (1988) 914-921.

14. *Trinity, Incarnation, and Atonement,* 31.

15. *The Crucified God: The Cross of Christ as the Foundation and Criticism of Christian Theology* (New York: Harper & Row, 1974); *The Way of Jesus Christ: Christology in Messianic Dimensions* (San Francisco: Harper San Francisco, 1990).

16. *The Crucified God,* 7, 72, 204. The role of the Spirit is developed more fully in Moltmann's later writings. Adapting Joachim of Fiore's Trinitarian view of the progressive phases of the kingdom in history, Moltmann sees successive kingdoms of the Father, the Son, and the Spirit in world history (*The Trinity and the Kingdom,* 209-212).

17. *God Was in Christ: An Essay on Incarnation and Atonement* (London: Faber, 1958, expanded edition 1963).

18. The doctrine found a vigorous advocate in the nineteenth century German Lutheran, Gottfried Thomasius, who saw in it a way of answering charges that the orthodox view of Jesus was unrealistic and unhistorical. *Kenosis* found a wider public in the English-speaking world through A.B. Bruce's *The Humiliation of Christ* (1881). The Anglican Charles Gore used it to explain Jesus' ignorance of biblical criticism, and later as a key to understanding God's self-limitation in dealing with human beings. Many have felt like Baillie that the doctrine raised more problems than it solved. Nevertheless, it has found recent advocates in S.W. Sykes, "The Strange Persistence of Kenotic Christology," in Alistair Kee and Eugene T. Long, eds., *Being and Truth: Essays in Honour of John Macquarrie* (London: S.C.M. Press, 1986) 349-375; Ronald J. Feenstra, "Reconsidering Kenotic Christology," in Feenstra and Plantinga, eds., *Trinity, Incarnation, and Atonement,* 128-152; and Gerald F. Hawthorne, *The Presence and the Power: The Significance of the Holy Spirit in the Life and Ministry of Jesus* (Dallas: Word, 1991) 199-226. Hawthorne sees the Spirit as the key insofar as the Spirit by whom Jesus was conceived and who anointed him at his baptism makes *kenosis* possible.

19. *God Was in Christ,* 115-132.

20. *Der christliche Glaube,* #94, 2: 43 (author's translation); cf. Baillie, *God Was in Christ,* 147.

21. G.W.H. Lampe, "The Holy Spirit and the Person of Christ," in S.W. Sykes and J.P. Clayton, eds., *Christ, Faith and History: Cambridge Studies in Christology* (Cambridge: Cambridge University Press, 1972) 111-130; Lampe, *God as Spirit,* The Bampton Lectures, 1976 (Oxford: Clarendon Press, 1977), see especially 61-94, 206-228.

22. *Christology in the Making: A New Testament Inquiry into the Origins of the Incarnation* (Philadelphia: Westminster Press, 1980) 138; cf. also Dunn, *Jesus and the Spirit: A Study of the Religious and Charismatic Experience of Jesus and the First Christians as Reflected in the New Testament* (Philadelphia: Westminster Presss, 1975) 92.

23. *Christology in the Making,* 138 (Dunn's italics).

24. *Cur deus homo* 1,4.

25. A number of scholars have pointed out that the Hebrew word for Spirit (*ruach* = breath, wind) is feminine. Perhaps the most consistent exponent of the idea of the Spirit as the divine Mother is Donald L. Gelpi, *The Divine Mother: A Trinitarian Theology of the Holy Spirit* (Lanham: University Press of America,1984); and *God Breathes the Spirit in the World* (Wilmington: Michael Glazier, 1988). Moltmann sees the imagery of motherhood in the language of being born of the Spirit (John 1: 12-13), and Mary as "a symbolic embodiment and as the human form of the Holy Spirit, who is the eternally virginal and divine mother of Christ" (*The Way of Jesus Christ,* 83).

26. *Trinity, Incarnation, and Atonement,* 32.

27. *Christology in the Making,* 62 (Dunn's italics).

28. For further discussion see (e.g.) C.F.D. Moule, *The Origin of Christology* (Cambridge: Cambridge University Press, 1977) 22-31; Martin Hengel, *The Son of God: The Origin of Christology and the History of Jewish-Hellenistic Religion* (London: S.C.M. Press, 1976); Dunn, *Christology in the Making,* 12-64; Marinus de Jonge, *Christology in Context: The Earliest Christian Response to Jesus* (Philadelphia: Westminster Press, 1988); Nils Alstrup Dahl, *Jesus the Christ: The Historical Origins of Chris-*

tological Doctrine (Minneapolis: Fortress Press, 1991) 113-136.

29. Op. cit., 28.

30. Colin Brown, *International Standard Bible Encyclopedia* 4.788-789. My understanding of the term is indebted to D.J.A. Clines, "The Image of God in Man," *Tyndale Bulletin* 19 (1968) 53-103, where Clines explores the background of the term in ancient Near Eastern literature. Images were believed to be the locus of the spirit of the deity. The idea of the pharaoh or the Babylonian king as the representative of a deity is well attested in Egyptian and Mesopotamian literature. In the OT it is not such kings but Adam, man as the image of God, who is God's representative endowed with authority to govern the earth (Gen 1: 26-30; cf. Psalm 8). As the Son of Man (or Son of Adam) Christ is given this authority.

31. Colin Brown, *That You May Believe, Miracles and Faith, Then and Now* (Grand Rapids: Eerdmans, 1985) 104-107; Moltmann, *The Way of Jesus Christ*, 212-227.

32. This seems to be the method followed by I. Howard Marshall in "The Divine Sonship of Jesus," *Jesus the Saviour: Studies in New Testament Theology* (Downers Grove: InterVarsity Press, 1990) 134-149. Linking Wis 2: 18 ("If the righteous man is God's son, he will help him, and will deliver him from the hand of his adversaries") with Jesus' resurrection, Marshall concludes that "the resurrection was the vindication of the status which Jesus had already claimed for himself" (p. 146). He goes on to reaffirm that "the roots of the New Testament designation of Jesus as the Son lie in his own consciousness of being uniquely related to the Father, a consciousness which he expressed both by speaking of God as 'my Father' and by referring to himself as 'the Son.'" However, this falls well short of social Trinitarian claims.

33. See (e.g.) Plantinga, *International Standard Bible Encyclopedia* 4. 915-916.

34. See the strictures of Joseph A. Fitzmyer on traditional Catholic exegesis in his *Scripture and Christology: A Statement of the Biblical Commission with a Commentary* (New York/Mahwah: Paulist Press, 1986) 60; T.E. Pollard, "The Exegesis of John x.30 in the Early Trinitarian Controversies," *New Testament Studies* 3 (1956-57); 334-349.

35. Note the wry comment of Raymond E. Brown: "It seems worth while to pause for a moment to summarize what we have heard thus far in John about the relations between Father and Son. The Son comes from the Father (viii 42); yet the Father who sent him is with him (viii 29). The Father loves the Son (iii 35); the Son knows the Father intimately (viii 55, x 15). In his mission on earth, the Son can do only what he has seen the Father do (v 19), can judge and speak only as he hears from the Father (v 30). The Son was taught from the Father (viii 28) and has received from Him powers such as that of judgment (v 22) and of giving and possessing life (v 21, 26, vi 57). The Son does the will of the Father (iv 34, vi 38) and has received a command from the Father that concerns his death and resurrection (x 18). *It will be noted that all these relationships between Father and Son are described in function of the Son's dealings with men. It would be the work of later theologians to take this gospel material pertaining to the mission of the Son ad extra and draw from it a theology of the inner life of the Trinity,*" *The Gospel according to John [i-xii]*, Anchor Bible (Garden City, NY: Doubleday, 1966) 407, italics mine.

36. See Plantinga in *Trinity, Incarnation, and Atonement*, 28; ISBE 4.915.

37. Hippolytus, *Contra Noetum*, Text introduced, edited and translated by Robert Butterworth (London: Heythrop Monographs, 1977) #15, p. 80; cf. Tertullian, *Against Hermogenes* 3.

38. Maurice Wiles, "Eternal Generation," in *Working Papers in Doctrine* (London: S.C.M. Press, 1976) 18-27. The passages personify wisdom in the created order as a woman who is prior to all other things.

39. *De Principiis* 1, 2, 1-6; cf. J.N.D. Kelly, *Early Christian Doctrines* (New York: Harper & Row, rev. ed. 1978) 128-132.

40. Kelly, *Early Christian Doctrines*, 121-123.

41. *Institutes* 2, 13, 4 (p 481).

42. 1 *Apology* 5, 4; 2 *Apology* 10, 1.

43. *Dialogue with Trypho* 61. See further Kelly, *Early Christian Doctrines*, 96-98, 110-112; Robert M. Grant, *Greek Apologists of the Second Century* (Philadelphia: Westminster Press, 1988) 600-61;

Grant, *Jesus after the Gospels: the Christ of the Second Century* (Louisville: Westminster/John Knox Press, 1990) 54-67.

44. See Dunn, *Christology in the Making,* 26-29.

45. Dunn, *Christology in the Making,,* 113-125; John Macquarrie, *Jesus Christ in Modern Thought* (Philadelphia: Trinity Press International, 1990) 56-59; Robert M. Grant, *Jesus after the Gospels,.* 28-29; James Wm. McClendon, Jr., Philippians 2: 5-11," *Review and Expositor* 88?4 (1991) 439-444. For background see Ralph P. Martin, *Carmen Christi: Philippians ii. 5-11 in Recent Interpretation and the Setting in Christian Worship* (revised edition Grand Rapids: Eerdmans, 1983) 161-164; N.T. Wright, *The Climax of the Covenant* (Edinburgh: T. & T. Clark, 1991) 56-98. Wright takes "a thing to be grasped" to mean holding on to something that one possesses already, and hence pre-existence. However, it could refer to the messianic sonship which Jesus already had in virtue of his anointing by the Spirit. Thus it would fit the interpretation given above.

46. Colin Brown, *Jesus in European Protestant Thought, 1778-1860* (reprint Grand Rapids: Baker Book House, 1988); "Synoptic Miracle Stories: A Jewish Religious and Social Setting," *Foundations and Facets Forum* 2 (1986) 56-76; *History and Faith: A Personal Exploration* (Grand Rapids: Zondervan, 1987); "Person of Christ," *The International Standard Bible Encyclopedia* 3 (1986) 781-801; *"Scripture and Christology: A Protestant Look at the Work of the Pontifical Biblical Commission,"* in Marguerite Shuster and Richard A. Muller, eds., *Perspectives in Christology: Essays in Honor of Paul K. Jewett* (Grand Rapids: Zondervan, 1991) 39-76; "Historical Jesus" in I. Howard Marshall et al., eds., *Dictionary of Jesus and the Gospels* (Downers Grove: InterVarsity Press, to be published in 1992).

47. Earl R. MacCormac, *Metaphor and Myth in Science and Religion* (Durham, North Carolina: Duke University Press, 1976) vii.

48. Both books published in Grand Rapids by Eerdmans. A revised expanded edition of *Miracles and the Critical Mind* is planned for publication by Baker Book House.

49. R.P.C. Hanson, *The Search for the Christian Doctrine of God,* 109-110, 562-572.

50. The Greek word *christos* and the Hebrew *mashiach* both mean "anointed." Initially, when the term was applied to Jesus it probably simply meant "the anointed one" (Anthony Harvey, *Jesus and the Constraints of History,* Bampton Lectures 1980 (Philadephia: Westminster Press, 1982) 80-82, 139-143, 149-153; John A.T. Robinson, *The Priority of John,* ed. J.F. Coakley (London: S.C.M. Press, 1985) 206. Inevitably, the designation of Jesus as "the anointed one" raises the question "By what or by whom was he anointed?" The answer of the Gospels is to link the prophecies of Isa 41: 1 and Isa 61: 1 to the baptism of Jesus and his subsequent anointing by the Spirit. Thus the term "Christ" carries with it not only an explicit reference to Jesus, but also an implicit reference to the Spirit.

51. The idea of the agent plays a significant part in Scripture and rabbinic thought. The rabbis used the term *shaliach,* and maintained that "a man's agent is as himself." See further Jan A. Buhner, *Der Gesandte und sein Weg im 4. Evangelium. Die kultur- und religionsgeschichtlichen Grundlagen der johanneischen Sendungschristologie sowie ihre traditionsgeschichtliche Entwicklickung,* WUNT 2. Reihe 2 (Tübingen: J.C.B. Mohr [Paul Siebeck], 1977); Peder Borgen, *Bread from Heaven: An Exegetical Study of the Concept of Manna in the Gospel of John and the Writings of Philo,* Supplements to Novum Testamentum 10 (Leiden: Brill, 1965) 158-164; Borgen, "God's Agent in the Fourth Gospel," in *Logos Was the True Light and Other Essays on the Gospel of John,* Relieff 9 (Trondheim: Tapir, 1983) 121-132; Howard Clark Kee, *What Can We Know about Jesus?* (Cambridge: Cambridge University Press, 1990) 104-110; Ben Witherington, III, *The Christology of Jesus* (Minneapolis: Fortress Press, 1990) 142-143.

52. Matt 11: 18-19 par. Luke 7: 33-35; Matt 11: 25-26 par. Luke 10: 21; Matt 11: 27 par. Luke 20: 22; Matt 12: 41-42 par. Luke 11: 31-32; Matt 23: 34-47 par. Luke 11: 49-51; 13: 34-35. Because Jesus is the wisdom of God incarnate, he can issue wisdom's invitation to come and take his yoke (Matt 11: 28-30; cf. Sir 51: 23-27). See further M. Jack Suggs, *Wisdom, Christology, and Law in Matthew's Gospel* (Cambridge, MA: Harvard University Press, 1970); R.G. Hamerton-Kelly, *Pre-Existence, Wisdom and the Son of Man: A Study of the Ideas of Pre-Existence in the New Testament,* SNTS Monographs 21 (Cambridge: Cambridge University Press, 1973); James M. Robinson, "Jesus as Sophos and Sophia: Wisdom Tradition and the Gospels," in Robert L. Wilken, ed., *Aspects of Wisdom in Judaism and Early*

Christianity (Notre Dame: University of Notre Dame Press, 1975) 1-16.

It may be noted that, whereas Logos is masculine, Sophia (wisdom) is feminine, and is frequently depicted as such. This and other considerations suggest to me that we should not identify the members of the Trinity with one or other sex (i.e., say with Gelpi and others that the Spirit is female as a counterpart to the maleness of the First and Second Persons of the Trinity). Rather, there is a sense in which the persons of the Trinity transcend sexuality and at the same time embody elements contained in sexual imagery.

53. Raymond E. Brown, *John*, 1, cxxii-cxxv.

Forsaking A Theology Of Glory
I Corinthians 1:18-31

MOLLY T. MARSHALL

If I appreciated country music (and I must confess, I do not), I would write a second verse to Mickey Gilley's "Looking for Love in All the Wrong Places." My verse would describe "Looking for God in All the Wrong Places." In this important passage on the doctrine of the cross, Paul warns Christians of the folly of looking in the wrong places for God while stumbling over the cross, the place of God's self-disclosure. He also reminds the Corinthian church (and the churches who will follow) that all persons may have access to knowledge of God if they are willing to forsake worldly wisdom.

The Apostle Paul carefully delineates the differences between God's wisdom and the wisdom of the world in this programmatic text. The wisdom of the world will not find God because God's power has been manifested in a most unlikely way—a way sure to cause sneers and humiliation in every age—Christ nailed to the cross. That is the proper place to look for God, Paul instructs, not in "signs" sure to convince or "wisdom" of human origin. To demand signs "implies refusal to take God on trust," according to C.K. Barrett.[1] Further, even though Paul knows this "word of the cross" is folly to those who are perishing, he exhorts "those who are being saved" to preach only Christ crucified. From experience he knew how difficult this was for proud and upright persons; the cross had been a scandal to him, too, at one time. Prior to his conversion, it was unthinkable for him to set aside the Law as God's means of righteousness.[2] Now, convinced of the power of the gospel, he proclaims it in all its starkness. He does not attempt to rival the eloquence of Apollos (v. 12), "lest the cross of Christ be emptied of its power" (v. 17).

This scandalous knowledge of God hurts, for it pierces all human presumptiveness. One has no basis for bargaining with God, no righteousness of one's own to claim. One can only stand with open, empty hands, in the posture of neediness and receptivity. God meets believing persons in the death of Christ, displaying that the "foolishness of God is wiser than human wisdom, and the weakness of God is stronger than that of humanity." God's radical presence is found in the last place the world would want to look, in a crucified messiah.[3] And Christians are to preach nothing else.

Such preaching cannot help but reorient our thoughts about God and about ourselves. What we believe to be the truth about God directly affects what we believe to be true about ourselves. The one who can only speak of God as impassible *Pantrocator*, untouched by the threats of human living, is usually overly impressed by the exalted nature of his or her own life and ministry. This one is not much interested in humble, unnoticed service; rather, all ministry has to be accompanied by triumphant fanfare and enthusiastic approbation. Members of the clergy are regrettably more vulnerable to an inflated self-assessment; members of the laity often make the opposite mistake of thinking too little of themselves and their contribution to the life of the church.

In verses 26-31 Paul offers a corrective to these misconceptions. He suggests that humility is the proper demeanor of the Christian. Those whom God has chosen to bear witness to the salvation found in Christ cannot boast in personal accomplishment or social standing. "God chose what is low and despised in the world, even things that are not, to bring to nothing things that are, so that no human being might boast in the presence of God" (vv. 28-29).

Here, in Paul's letter to the Corinthians, we catch an echo of the "eschatological reversal"[4] characteristic of the parables and predictions of Jesus. Status and expectations, as the world now knows them, will be turned upside down as the reign of God is fully demonstrated. Already God is using those with little acclaim for redemptive purposes. The Christian community at Corinth was comprised of slaves and freed persons; few enjoyed the privileges of wealth or noble birth.

In the climax to this passage (vv. 30-31), Paul carefully links God's salvific work in Christ to the life of the Christian. God is the very "source of your life in Christ Jesus," he affirms. Clearly he is proclaiming that Christians have no life apart from life in Christ; before their belief, they could be counted among "things that are not" (v. 28). Murphy-O'Connor interprets this expression to mean: "Only those who are in Christ exist as God intended them to exist, for only they can love creatively in freedom."[5] This affirmation can enable us to know our proper significance and continuing dependence.

Martin Luther perhaps best understood what Paul was saying. His distinction between "theology of glory" and "theology of the cross" is strikingly similar to Paul's contrast between the fraudulent wisdom of humanity and the "foolish wisdom of God." In a day characterized by papal and ecclesiastical excesses, Luther was also concerned that Christians might look for God in the wrong places. In the *Heidelberg Disputation* of 1518,[6] he warns his hearers of this error by reminding them of God's display of power in the cross. Those who cling to the wisdom of the world are affirming a theology of glory, Luther argues. The theology of glory seeks to know God directly in the obviously divine power and wisdom of glorious Holy Being; it presumes to be capable of perceiving clearly God's transcendent, majestic reign. The theology of the cross, paradoxically, recognizes God precisely where God has chosen to hide, in suffering and in all that the wisdom of the world considers to be weakness and folly. Recently a student in my theology class asked why people seem to think God is better represented by strong, healthful persons rather than those with broken health and creaking joints. His question was most perceptive. I was reminded of Brian Wren's hymn, "Bring Many Names,"[7] which pictures God as old and aching, "grey with endless care." The God whom the cross discloses reveals strength in such seemingly abysmal weakness.

The theology of glory leads one to stand before God and attempt to justify oneself on the basis of ethical or intellectual achievements. Paul had learned of the bankruptcy of such endeavor.[8] So had Luther. Conversely, the theology of the cross considers the Christian to be one who has been called to suffer in the hiddenness where God works. Indeed, we have been called to participate in what the world will hardly notice.[9] These words of Paul, given new hearing by Luther, sound strange to an era characterized by a theology of glory. It is a national mood, you know. Movies such as "Top Gun" and "The

Terminator" (*ad nauseam)* fan the flames of our triumphalism. Our military security demands more and more instruments of destruction. Our swagger following Desert Storm only underscores our preoccupation with might. The theologian of glory is quite sure that God is humming (the bass part, of course) "The Battle Hymn of the Republic" right alongside.

A theology of glory marks our ecclesial life as well. We do not really have much room for the God revealed in the helplessness of the cross, do we? The power of personal orthodoxy, the power of the size of the dynasty being built, the power of demagogic authority, the power of economic security—these seem to be, in the minds of many, the mark of God's favorable identification with the success syndrome of church life today. In my own denomination there is little room for nonwhite, female, or handicapped persons as a visible part of our Southern Baptist leadership.

There is no room in the theology of glory for the marginal, the broken, the "bruised reeds" (Isa 42:3), or even the servant who refuses to trumpet the message. There is no room for the one with serious questions, or, God forbid, *doubt;* there is no hospitable space for flickering faith, only clear bright fire. The theologian of glory lives vehemently with the presumption of grasping truth, without any mixture of error. This one forgets that "divine folly is wiser" than the wisdom he or she can generate. The theology of glory has little patience with the struggles of the Christian life. It refuses to admit that "the harbour of the convert is still troubled by storms," as Augustine confessed.

Elementary studies in psychology teach us what we refuse to acknowledge within us is quite often projected onto those who oppose us. If only *they* would see the light, we lament. But we cannot reshape others; that is God's work. We can only seek to be responsible for the integrity of our own position and trust God to work in the hearts of others. Thus, we must confront those aspects of a theology of glory that seduce us and allow them to be crucified with Christ.

First, we must be very reticent about co-opting God for our political or theological maneuverings. It is much easier to pretend God has sanctioned our vested interests than to look diligently for the hidden purposes of God. It is God's purposes that ultimately will enable us to look for God "in all the right places". . . the struggling pastor whose statistics impress no one; the quiet voice of sanity in the nation's capital; the humiliation of the homeless; and, perhaps most clearly, in the voluntary labor of common Christians in Vacation Bible School, Habitat for Humanity, literacy projects or the local nursing home. We must learn to make our home with God in these places.

Second, forsaking a theology of glory beckons us to humility. Our confidence must be found in Christ, not our own cleverness. This is a stumbling block to many in academic life as well as in church life. Not to know all the outcomes politically or eschatologically, requires us to trust. Only one who knows herself insufficient in herself has the humility to trust. Only he who realizes the hiddenness of God in the suffering of Christ and the groaning of all creation can patiently wait in hope for God's triumph. How desperately we all need a good dose of humility so that we might *trust God,* not our cleverness or ambitions but *God.*

Finally, forsaking a theology of glory allows us to embrace a new kind of strength. Its source is the power of suffering love which is ours in Christ.[10] God's power is always power in relationship and God shares power with us that we might be empowered for compassionate living. Our strength comes from God's weakness in our behalf. When we believe Christ's cross to be our own, our smug self-confidence is destroyed, our frantic competitiveness can be stilled, and we cling to Christ. We then can walk the pathway from moralistic activism to grace, allowing God's good work in us and through us for the sake of the perishing.

NOTES

1. C. K. Barrett, *The First Epistle to the Corinthians*, Harpers New Testament Commentaries (New York: Harper and Row, 1968) 54.

2. Christiaan Beker has a most helpful discussion of the role of the Law as an instrument of God. See his *Paul the Apostle: The Triumph of God in Life and Thought* (Philadelphia: Fortress, 1980) 235ff. Cf. E. P. Sanders' work, Paul and Palestinian Judaism (Philadelphia: Fortress, 1977) 474ff.

3. Peter Stuhlmacher offers an encompassing discussion of Paul's theology of the cross in his recent *Reconciliation, Law, and Righteousness* (Philadelphia: Fortress, 1986) 155ff.

4. This is Elisabeth Schussler Fiorenza's descriptive term explicating the inclusive nature of the *basileia* proclaimed by Jesus. See her work, *In Memory of Her: Feminist Theological Reconstruction of Christian Origins* (New York: Crossroad, 1983) 122. Rosemary Radford Ruether also pursues this theme in *Sexism and God-Talk: Toward Feminist Theology* (Boston: Beacon Press, 1983) 193ff.

5. Jerome Murphy-O'Connor, *1 Corinthians, New Testament Message*, 10 (Wilmington, Del.: Michael Glazier, Inc. 1979) 16.

6. WA1, 361 f; LW 31, 52. Theses 19 and 20 of the *Heidelberg Disputation*. Cf. Alister E. McGrath, *Luther's Theology of the Cross* (Oxford: Basil Blackwell, 1985).

7. Brian Wren, *Bring Many Names* (Carol Stream, Illinois: Hope Publishing Company, 1989).

8. W. D. Davies argues convincingly that Paul affirms Christ as the "New Torah," the Wisdom of God, in *Paul and Rabbinic Judaism*, 4th ed. (Philadelphia: Fortress, 1980) 147ff.

9. Donald P. McNeill, Douglas A. Morrison, and Henri J. M. Nouwen probe the character of this kind of Christian obedience in *Compassion: Reflection on the Christian Life* (Garden City, N.Y.: Image Books, 1983).

10. A critical concern of contemporary theological reflection is the significance of God's suffering. See Warren McWilliams' survey of the resurgence of theopaschite theology in *The Passion of God: Divine Suffering in Contemporary Protestant Theology* (Macon: Mercer Press, 1985). For further study in this area, see Leonardo Boff, *Passion of Christ, Passion of World* (Maryknoll: Orbis, 1987); Arthur C. McGill, *Suffering: Test of Theological Method* (Philadelphia: Westminster Press, 1982); and, of course, the work by Jürgen Moltmann, *The Crucified God* (New York: Harper and Row, 1974).

THE CONTRIBUTORS

COLIN BROWN
Fuller Theological Seminary - Pasadena, CA

BALMER H. KELLY
Union Theological Seminary in Virginia - Richmond, VA

RALPH KLEIN
Lutheran School of Theology at Chicago - Chicago, IL

I. HOWARD MARSHALL
University of Aberdeen - Aberdeen, Scotland

MOLLY T. MARSHALL
Southern Baptist Theological Seminary - Louisville, KY

JAMES LUTHER MAYS
Union Theological Seminary in Virginia - Richmond, VA

LAWRENCE MURPHY
Garrett-Evangelical Theological Seminary - Evanston, IL

FRED NORRIS
Emmanuel School of Religion - Johnson City, TN

THOMAS WRIGHT
Worcester College - Oxford, England

Professors of Biblical Theology

Have you considered using the issues of EX AUDITU as basic resources for your Seminars in Biblical Theology?

EX AUDITU Vol. 1 (1985) consists of selected articles presenting the issues inherent in the theological interpretation of Scripture.

EX AUDITU Vol. 2 (1986) discusses the theme: "Church and State Relationship." In addition there are two lead articles, one by Peter Stuhlmacher on "EX AUDITU and the Theological Interpretation of Holy Scripture," and the second by Ben F. Meyer on "The Primacy of Consent and the Uses of Suspicion."

EX AUDITU Vol. 3 (1987). The theme is: "Creation."

EX AUDITU Vol. 4 (1988). The theme is: "The Church and Israel (Romans 9-11)."

EX AUDITU Vol. 5 (1989). The theme is: "What is Salvation?"

EX AUDITU Vol. 6 (1990). The theme is: "Prophetic and/or Apocalyptic Eschatology."

EX AUDITU Vol. 7 (1991). The theme is: "Christology and Incarnation."

EX AUDITU Vol. 8 (1992). to be published in the Spring of 1993 will be on the theme: "Worship."

Ten copies or more may be purchasedfor $10.00 per copy from:

Pickwick Publications
4137 Timberlane Drive
Allison Park, PA 15101-2932

PICKWICK PUBLICATIONS

4137 Timberlane Drive
Allison Park, PA 15101-2932

Critical Realism and the New Testament
By Ben F. Meyer
ISBN 0-915138-97-2 $19.95

The Epigones: A Study of the Theology of the Genevan Academy at the Time of the Synod of Dort
By William A. McComish
ISBN 0-915138-62-X $36.00

Social Concern in Calvin's Geneva
By William C. Innes
ISBN 0-915138-33-6 $19.95

Freedom and Civilization Among The Greeks
By A. J. Festugière
Tr. by P. T. Brannan
ISBN 0-915138-98-0 $15.00

The Kitchen Saint and the Heritage of Islam: Conversations, Spiritual Maxims and Letters of Brother Lawrence
Tr. by Elmer H. Douglas
ISBN 1-55635-003-1 $10.00

Luke the Theologian. Thirty-three years of Research (1950-1983)
By François Bovon
ISBN 0-915138-93-X $35.00

The Present and the Past
A Study of Anamnesis
By Richard J. Ginn
ISBN 1-55635-004-X $12.00

Searching for Lost Coins
Explorations in Christianity and Feminism
By Ann Loades
ISBN 1-55635-000-7 $12.00

Theology Beyond Christendom. Essays on the Centenary of the Birth of Karl Barth
Ed. by John Thompson
ISBN 915138-85-9 $29.95

A Theology of Electricity
By Ernst Benz
Tr. by Dennis Stillings
ISBN 0-915138-92-1 $19.95

The Triune God. An Ecumenical Study
By E. L. Mascall
(Co-published with Churchman Publishing)
ISBN 0-915138-96-4 $12.90

The Quest for Church Unity
From John Calvin to Isaac d'Huisseau
By Richard Stauffer
ISBN 0-915138-63-8 $15.00

The Will of God and the Cross
An Historical and Theological Study of John Calvin's Doctrine of Limited Redemption
By Jonathan H. Rainbow
ISBN 1-55635-005-8 $24.00

Anselm: Fides Quaerens Intellectum
Anselm's proof of the existence of God in the context of his theological scheme
By Karl Barth
ISBN 0-915138-75-1 $15.00

The Holy Spirit in the Theology of Karl Barth
By John Thompson
ISBN 0-915138-94-8 $24.00

God With Us
By Joseph Haroutunian
A Theology of Transpersonal Life
ISBN 1-55635-008-2 $19.95

Jeshua: Nazareth to Jerusalem
By Moelwyn Merchant
ISBN 1-55635-010-4 $24.00

Christ In Our Place
By T. Hart & D. Thimell
ISBN 1-55635-009-0 $35.00

Gladstone: The Making of a Christian Politician (1809-1832)
By Peter J. Jagger $24.00